WHAT TO SAY *and* HOW TO SAY IT

Volume 2

More Ways to Discuss Your Faith
with Clarity and Confidence

"If you long to have charitable conversations about hot-button issues with friends and loved ones, this book is for you. If you want to be equipped to defend Church teaching with logical reasoning and avoid a heated argument, Brandon Vogt can be your guide. He takes you step-by-step through some of the most emotionally charged topics of today so you can find common ground with those who disagree and communicate truth with clarity and kindness."

Haley Stewart
Author of *The Grace of Enough*

WHAT TO SAY *and* HOW TO SAY IT

Volume 2

More Ways to Discuss Your Faith with Clarity and Confidence

BRANDON VOGT

A 💡 *Claritas*U Book

Ave Maria Press · AVE · Notre Dame, Indiana

Founded in 1865, Ave Maria Press is a ministry of the United States Province of Holy Cross.

www.avemariapress.com

Paperback: ISBN-13 978-1-64680-049-0

E-book: ISBN-13 978-1-64680-050-6

Cover and text design by Andy Wagoner.

Printed and bound in Canada.

Library of Congress Cataloging-in-Publication Data is available.

CONTENTS

ACKNOWLEDGMENTS

First of all, I would like to thank the whole Ave Maria Press team for their talent, encouragement, and excitement about this book series. You never fail to impress! Partnering with you has been nothing but pleasant.

Special appreciation goes to Bert Ghezzi, my longtime friend and cheerful editor, who helped shape this book into something that makes sense. You deserve credit for any good sentences that appear.

I must thank Bishop Robert Barron, Fr. Steve Grunow, and the whole Word on Fire team for demonstrating "affirmative orthodoxy," showing how to effectively present the beauty and truth of Catholicism to a world that largely dismisses it.

Finally, this book has been adapted from courses inside ClaritasU, so I can't help but thank the thousands of ClaritasU students who have shaped these lessons and strategies over the years. Your impact is all over this book, and your interactions and feedback have made it far better. Special thanks go to John DeRosa, whose many gifts, both intellectually and technically, have helped ClaritasU to flourish.

INTRODUCTION

In the introduction to the first book in this series, *What to Say and How to Say It*, I shared the results of a recent Pew Research Forum study which found that only 2 percent of Catholics were open to discussing their religious views with people who disagree. In other words, 98 percent of Catholics preferred to just listen to other peoples' religious beliefs (never sharing their own) or avoid discussing religion altogether. These depressing results earned Catholics the designation of being the *least likely group* to discuss their religious beliefs with others. People from every other faith tradition—Protestants, Jews, Muslims, Buddhists, and even atheists and agnostics—were more willing to discuss their religious views.

After reading those survey results, I remember wondering, "How would St. Peter react to this?" Peter, remember, encouraged Christians to "always be ready to give an explanation to anyone who asks you for a reason for your hope" (1 Pt 3:15). He could hardly be clearer: Christians are meant to be ready to openly discuss our faith, to explain our beliefs to people who don't understand them. Of course, he adds, we should "do it with gentleness and reverence." Peter was not advocating that we scream or shove our views down others' throats. But he does encourage us to calmly, charitably, and reasonably explain why we believe what we do.

That's what this book will teach you. As in the first volume of this series, this book covers seven hot-button topics that Catholics typically avoid in conversation. These are issues that make most Catholics nervous, tongue-tied, and afraid, the ones they hope never turn up in discussion. For each topic, you'll get clear on the Catholic view on the issue, the best objections to that view (so you're not surprised when encountering them in real-life conversations), and finally how to answer those objections with clarity and confidence. By the end of the book, you'll no longer be part of the 98 percent that avoids these topics. You'll become part of the small, poised minority that is no longer afraid.

The first chapter focuses on faith and science. For many people, especially the young, this is the biggest stumbling block to faith. Have you ever heard someone claim science has disproven God, or that the Church hates science, or that we must choose between either religion or science? Learn what to say in this chapter.

We'll then turn to Jesus' Resurrection in chapter 2. You'll learn a proven strategy for showing even the most skeptical observers that we have good reasons for believing Jesus rose from the dead, that his Resurrection is not just a historical myth or wish-fulfillment fantasy.

In chapter 3, you'll learn how to discuss the Last Things, particularly heaven, hell, and purgatory. Much confusion exists around these three eternal states, which you'll discover not only among nonbelievers but also fellow Christians. This chapter will help you navigate through the fog.

In the fourth, fifth, and sixth chapters, we'll look at three of the most pressing challenges to Catholics today: relativism, Islam, and homosexuality. Most Catholics don't want to touch any of these topics with a ten-foot pole. But as you'll see, it's not difficult to understand these topics and learn how to defend the Church's positions on each one, with sensitivity and persuasion.

Finally, we'll close the book with a chapter on Mary, often the biggest hurdle for Protestant Christians who are considering the Catholic faith. Finishing the book this way follows a long tradition in the Church of concluding formal documents, whether they be papal encyclicals or teachings from a council, with a reflection on the Mother of God. So, it's a fitting conclusion here.

Each of the chapters in this book is based on a video course we've offered at ClaritasU, my online membership platform for Catholics, and has been adapted for this book. If you like the format of these chapters and the tips and strategies they include, you'll love ClaritasU, which offers even *more* tactics and resources on even *more* hot-button issues. Learn more and join the thousands of Catholics getting clear about their faith at ClaritasU.com.

Let's dive in!

1

FAITH AND SCIENCE

Many Christians are leery about science, but I've long been interested in it. In college I majored in engineering and minored in physics. Even today, one of my passions is dialoguing with science-minded atheists and skeptics.

Whatever your own history with science, the fact is that the so-called "conflict" between faith and science is pressing, especially since many people who reject Christianity do so on the basis on science. We have to get clear about this topic if we are going to talk about our faith with confidence. So, in this chapter you will learn

- where the conflict between faith and science came from;
- how to respond to scientism;
- how to answer big myths, like "sciences disproves God";
- the truth about the Galileo affair; and
- why evolution is not a problem for Catholics.

You will finish this chapter with a sigh of relief, knowing you will never have to get rattled about faith and science again when the topic comes up in conversation.

THE ORIGIN OF THE CONFLICT BETWEEN FAITH AND SCIENCE

The obvious place to begin is with the question, "How did the notion that faith and science conflict arise?" Most historians trace this back to the Enlightenment, the eighteenth-century intellectual movement that aggressively opposed religion.

Enlightenment thinkers wanted to usher in a new Age of Reason in which rational thought alone—not God, the Bible, or the Church—was the ultimate source of authority. And to do this they needed to undermine the Catholic Church's extensive influence on society. The leaders of the Enlightenment achieved this by promoting a false dichotomy between faith and science. They contended that we had a choice: we could either blindly follow fixed Catholic dogmas, or we could use reason to figure things out ourselves through scientific experimentation. Therefore, everyone must decide between either faith or reason, either religion or science, but we can't have both.

Over the last three centuries that false choice has taken root deep in our culture. Today, you see it prominently among two extreme groups. On the one hand, the New Atheists—people such as Richard Dawkins and the late Stephen Hawking—promote the sciences as a more enlightened alternative to religion. On the other extreme, many fundamentalist Protestants dismiss science as an unreliable, anti-religious conspiracy. Both groups, science lovers who dismiss religion and religion lovers who dismiss science, have caused many people today to think faith and science are interminably at odds.

But this is not just a problem on the extremes. When you look at surveys asking former Catholics why they left the Church, inevitably the word *science* pops up in the responses.

Dr. Christian Smith, a leading Catholic sociologist, recently carried out an extensive study of young adults who were raised Catholic but are no longer Catholic today. He made this observation: "This idea came up again and again in our interviews: science and logic are how we really know things about our world, and religious faith either violates or falls short of the standard of scientific knowledge."[1]

Look at this chart from Dr. Smith's report. Researchers asked young people whether they agreed or disagreed with this statement: "The teachings of science and religion often ultimately conflict with each other." Here's what they said:

AGREE OR DISAGREE: THE TEACHINGS OF SCIENCE AND RELIGION OFTEN ULTIMATELY CONFLICT WITH EACH OTHER.
(PERCENTS)

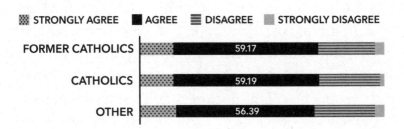

Notice that when you combine the "strongly agree" and the "agree" bars, you see that the overwhelming majority of young people—more than 75 percent—think faith and science are in conflict. Notice, too, that there's virtually no difference in the responses of former Catholics, Catholics, and non-Catholics. In other words, even young Catholics are convinced that faith and science are in opposition. In fact, you can see on the chart that young people raised Catholic were actually more likely than non-Catholics to believe in the conflict between faith and science!

As Dr. Smith notes, for many people today, "being scientific is seen as being smart, savvy, and realistic about the world we live in. Being religious, by implication, is seen as being gullible, naive, and weak."[2]

The Church and the Conflict between Faith and Science

But is this really the case? Well, before answering that question, it's worth considering what the Catholic Church actually teaches about science. For Catholics true faith and true science are never in conflict. They will never be in conflict because the truths of faith and the truths of science, if genuine, can never contradict each other. They both flow from God, the ground of all truth, and truth can't contradict truth.

St. John Paul II wrote a magnificent encyclical letter titled *Fides et Ratio*, which is Latin for "faith and reason." The opening line of the document brilliantly illustrates the Catholic view of science: "Faith and reason are like two wings on which the human spirit rises to the contemplation of truth."[3]

Picture a bird, lifting up into flight, both wings flapping together. The wings are not in conflict; rather, they're complementary. Both wings work together to rise up to the heights. The same relationship holds between faith and science. Catholics know that to rise to the full contemplation of truth, as the pope says, we need both wings flapping together in harmony.

Catholics don't shun science. We embrace it, we value it, and we promote it. We aren't afraid of science and have no problem with genuine scientific truths.

RESPONDING TO SCIENTISM

But then why do so many people think Christianity is incompatible with science? One reason is that appreciation for science often devolves into scientism, which is a very fashionable ideology today.

Defining Scientism

Scientism is the belief that all knowledge about reality—not just some knowledge but all—comes from what the hard sciences, especially physics and chemistry, have proven. Advocates of scientism believe science is the *only* trustworthy way to arrive at truth. Its advocates hold that all other claims, including those about God, morality, politics, beauty, and more, are merely expressions of private opinion or emotion.

You see this scientism in survey responses from former Christians, who often say things like, "Well, as I got older, I knew I had to choose between faith and science, since they're obviously incompatible, and since I trusted science so much, I had to give up faith." Others say something like, "Science is the only way to know what's true, objective, and reliable, and since faith isn't science, then we can't rely on it. It can't arrive at truth."

Now that you know what scientism is, you will start recognizing it everywhere. For example, on the bestseller rack at your local bookstore you will see a book championing how science unlocks the secrets to life. Or turn on the television or internet and you will find advocates of scientism speaking about science as reverently as any religious person does their faith. Or go to any college campus and you'll see science departments heralded above the rest, especially above the humanities, as the pinnacle of education.

Responding to Scientism

You can use two main strategies to respond to someone who advocates scientism. First, show how scientism is self-refuting. Here you want to demonstrate that it contradicts itself. Second, raise for discussion things we know are true but that science can't explain. Let's consider these approaches one at a time.

Scientism Refutes Itself

It's fairly easy to show that scientism is self-refuting. You can ask an advocate of scientism, "Are you saying that we should believe only what can be proved scientifically?" If they say, "Well, no . . ." then you can say, "Great! We agree, then, that there are other ways besides science to arrive at knowledge, such as religion, philosophy, the arts, moral reasoning, and more."

But if the person says, "Yes, we should only believe what can be proved scientifically," then you can ask, "Has it been proved scientifically that 'we should only believe what can be proved scientifically'? What scientific experiment proved that?"

Most likely the person will relent and admit that scientism is not scientifically provable. In that case, you've found agreement. You can affirm together that science is just one of many avenues to the truth, and that the supposed conflict between science and other sources of knowledge is just a myth.

By the way, you'll see we didn't use the word "scientism" in this exchange. You should note that most people who embrace scientism don't care for the label and take it negatively, as an insult. So, even if the person embraces scientism, don't use that term in conversations. Just discuss the idea, not the term.

Overall, your goal is to help the other person see why scientism is self-refuting, that it's impossible to prove scientifically that scientism is true. This is because scientism is not a scientific statement but a philosophy. It is not science itself, but it expresses a theoretical viewpoint *about* science. So, the only way to accept scientism is to recognize the validity of philosophy. Yet accepting philosophy undermines the whole claim of scientism, that science is the only way to truth. So, as you can see, there are multiple ways to achieve this goal in conversation, to show that scientism is self-refuting.

Truths that Science Can't Explain

A second way to refute scientism is to help the other person see that they hold truths we all embrace but that can't be explained scientifically.

My favorite example is morality. Virtually all of us believe in certain moral truths. For example, everyone holds that it's always wrong to torture babies for fun. No sane person would ever think it's ever acceptable to brutalize toddlers purely for entertainment purposes. But why is that true? It's certainly not a truth we derive from science. There's no experiment that can confirm it's wrong to torture children. We have to rely on other ways of reasoning such as moral intuition and philosophy, rather than chemistry or physics, to show that it's wrong. Specifically, we depend on the philosophy of ethics to demonstrate that all human beings have inviolable human dignity, which makes it wrong to harm them, especially innocent babies.

Once you persuade another person to see that we all hold to facts that aren't necessarily scientific, you've opened them to other ways of understanding the world besides science. This can help someone escape the shackles of the view that science explains everything.

With scientism behind us, we can move on to some of the other big myths that turn up when discussing faith and science.

ANSWERING THE BIG MYTHS

When someone tells you faith and science are at odds, you should ask for details. Ask the person to explain exactly how and why they are in conflict. In most cases, your conversation partner will mention one of a few common myths. Let's consider four of them and how to respond.

Myth 1: Science Has Disproven God

This myth doesn't just hold that religion is anti-scientific. It goes even further and argues that modern science has shown that God doesn't exist. However, in almost every case, when someone claims that science has disproved God, the God they're referring to is known as the "God of the gaps."

Before modern science, most ancient people attributed to gods all the mysterious phenomena they couldn't otherwise explain. For example, they wondered, "Why did our crops grow so well this year? Well, the gods must have been pleased! Why did we lose that war? Well, the gods must have been angry with us!"

This is known as the "God of the gaps," where a God (or set of gods) is used to fill in the gaps of our knowledge about the world. But over the centuries, as science developed and began to explain many of these phenomena through natural causes, the "God of the gaps" became smaller and smaller. We learned that crops grew well because of favorable weather. Wars were won or lost because of bad strategy and inadequate weapons. Thus, God was needed less and less to explain things.

Here's the important point: when people today say that "science has disproven God," the God they have in mind is almost always a "God of the gaps." They believe that because science can now explain everything that people once needed divine beings to explain, there is no need for God—he's been disproven. (Ignore, for the moment, the fact that even if we could explain everything without reference to God, it wouldn't follow that God doesn't exist.)

So, how should you respond to this? Two things are helpful. First, you want to acknowledge that you don't believe in God simply because you can't otherwise explain things in nature. Affirm that you have other strong reasons to believe in God (many of these are laid out in the first volume of *What to Say and How to Say It*.)

Second, you want to emphasize that God is not just one scientific hypothesis among many. He's not a material cause within the universe. Because God is immaterial and timeless, he is outside of space and time. Therefore, by definition, he *cannot* be a scientific explanation for the things because science only concerns *natural* explanations for *natural* phenomena, and God is *supernatural*. In other words, God is not just one more natural cause that might be discarded once we discover better natural causes; he's the very ground of existence, the reason why the natural world exists at all. So, God is not in competition with scientific explanations. He's responsible for there being a natural world at all, a world that science can measure and study.

Myth 2: Six Literal Days of Creation

The second myth says, "The Bible teaches the earth was created in six literal days, and science has shown that's false." Although some fundamentalist Protestants believe in this view, known as "six-day creationism," the Catholic Church doesn't affirm this interpretation of Genesis. (To be fair, some of the Church Fathers did hold a literal belief in six days of creation, but only a few, and that view has never been officially endorsed by the Church.)

In the fourth century, St. Augustine explained why six-day creationism doesn't make sense. Genesis says that God created light on day one but didn't create the sun until day four. For this reason, even many early Christians rejected the literalist reading of Genesis. So, you can dismiss the myth with this explanation and affirm that this just isn't what Catholics believe.

Myth 3: Most Scientists Are Atheists

A third myth holds that most scientists are atheists, so there must be an incompatibility between science and faith. This claim is less of an argument and more of a suggestion that because many smart people don't believe in God, we shouldn't either.

But is the claim true? Well, it is true that scientists are more likely to be atheists than believers. In *Science vs. Religion: What Scientists Really Think*, Elaine Ecklund concludes that while only 8 percent of the general population is atheist or agnostic, roughly 60 percent of science professors are. In other words, scientists are seven to eight times more likely to be atheist than the general population

But interestingly, after interviewing hundreds of scientists and analyzing lots of survey data, Ecklund also found that very few scientists lost their faith through science. Science didn't turn them into atheists. Most were atheist well before they began pursuing science, and it was their interest in the natural world that led them into the field.

Also, Ecklund's book verifies that few scientists have put much time into studying the best arguments for God or for Christianity. It's just not their specialty or focus. They may be smart in one field (science) but not necessarily in others (for example, religion.) Studies show that the people who *have* put in the effort to study the arguments for and against God, especially those working in the fields of philosophy of religion, tend overwhelmingly to be believers.

In any case, your main response to this myth should be to say, "Okay, but what's your point? Even if many scientists rejected God, that's not a great reason for us to reject him. Why think scientists are experts on the question of God?" For every contentious issue, whether it be politics, religion, morality, or even science, there are always really sharp people on both sides of the debate. So, the question shouldn't be, "Which side has more smart people?" The question should be, "Is the view true?" When you hear this myth, try to reroute the conversation away from what position "smart people" take, and instead focus on the actual arguments.

Myth 4: The Catholic Church Is Anti-Science

Let's look at one more myth: "The Catholic Church is anti-science. It's always standing against scientific progress." One response to this charge is to ask the person to get more specific. For instance, ask, "Is there something specific you have in mind? An example where the Church stood against science?" Then you can deal with that specific issue rather than this broad accusation.

However, my favorite strategy here is to introduce some of the many famous Catholic scientists, who by their very existence undermine this myth. For instance, if you conduct a Google search for "Catholic scientists," you will find lists including hundreds of famous Catholic scientists.

Of course, for your conversations you don't need to cite all those scientists' names. Just remembering two or three will be helpful. One of my favorites is Fr. Georges Lemaître, a Belgian priest and physicist. Lemaître formulated the Big Bang theory, which is the most popular theory about the origin of our universe. Notably, Fr. Lemaître had to convince Albert Einstein that his theory was true. Einstein initially disagreed with it, but Fr. Lemaître won him over. So, if someone tells you the Catholic Church is anti-science, you can say, "Well, if the Church hates science so much, how was it that a Catholic priest, Fr. Georges Lemaître, formulated the Big Bang theory?"

Here are two more Catholic scientists to remember. A Catholic priest, Fr. Gregor Mendel, is the father of modern genetics, and Franciscan friar Roger Bacon is the father of the scientific method.

We will deal with two other Big Myths later in this chapter—the Galileo affair and evolution.

Expert Interview with Stacy A. Trasancos

➤ **Watch the interview here: https://claritasu.com/trasancos**

Dr. Stacy A. Trasancos is a wife and homeschooling mother of seven. She holds a PhD in Chemistry and an MA in Dogmatic Theology. She was a senior research chemist for DuPont before converting to Catholicism. Dr. Trasancos is the author of two books, *Science Was Born of Christianity* and *Particles of Faith: A Catholic Guide to Navigating Science*. She serves as the executive director of the St. Philip Institute of Catechesis and Evangelization in the Diocese of Tyler, Texas.

In this interview, Dr. Trasancos responds to the following questions:

1. How did you first get interested in the convergence of faith and science?
2. Why do you think so many people presume that faith and science are in conflict?
3. Explain how science arose from a specifically Christian context.
4. What should Catholics know about evolution?
5. What are some big mistakes Catholics make when discussing issues of faith and science?
6. What are some talking points that Catholics should remember when discussing faith and science?

Excerpt from the Interview

"I've seen Catholics also say, 'I'm going to disregard science because I'm scared of it, I don't like what it's saying. I'm just going to stick to the faith.' The big answer, the full answer, which is what the Catholic Church is all about, is that we need both. Science is the study of the handiwork of God. And once you understand that, then you're free to explore science, all of it, in every detail. Even the theories that seem questionable, you're free to explore them looking for the truth. And you're also free to be completely grounded in your faith. You need that full picture, both ways." (Stacy A. Trasancos)

THE GALILEO AFFAIR

The Galileo affair is one of the oldest myths surrounding the conflict between faith and science.

The story is legendary. In the seventeenth century, Galileo Galilei was a gifted astronomer who made the earth-shaking discovery that instead of the sun and other planets rotating around the earth (a view known as geocentrism) the earth and other planets actually rotated around the sun (a view known as heliocentrism).

However, the Church didn't like his conclusions because the Bible taught that the sun revolved around the earth. It demanded that Galileo renounce his scientific discoveries. When he refused to do so, the Church had him tortured and imprisoned until he recanted this heretical belief.

Does that story sound familiar? Have you seen that narrative repeated on blogs, websites, television shows, and across the culture? It's become one of the "origin stories" of modern science, and the account of this bold scientist's martyrdom by the bullying, irrational Church is usually the number one example people give to show how faith and science are locked in irresolvable conflict.

The problem with this myth is that most of it is untrue. At best, the details are wildly exaggerated. Let's unpack the story piece by piece.

First, the Catholic Church did not condemn Galileo's science. It did not denounce his heliocentric view of the universe. The Church doesn't make pronouncements on scientific issues like that. In fact, ninety years before Galileo's trial, Nicolaus Copernicus, a Polish mathematician and astronomer, wrote a book defending heliocentrism that was celebrated by many churchmen (Copernicus even dedicated the book to the pope). The Church never condemned heliocentrism, and Galileo was not even the first proponent of that theory; Copernicus is credited with that.

Second, most churchmen believed in geocentrism during Galileo's time, but not because they held a literalistic reading of the Bible. They believed in geocentrism because it was the default scientific view of the period. Most scientists of the early seventeenth century were geocentrists, due to arguments made by Aristotle and because the scientific evidence available at the time seemed to support geocentrism.

So, to be clear, this was not a case of a backward-thinking Church rejecting the scientific consensus. In reality, Galileo was proposing a new theory that *overturned* the mainstream view of science.

This brings us to the third point: instead of rejecting Galileo's heliocentrism, the Church only urged him to proceed cautiously and not to overstate his case given the revolutionary nature of his theory. Pope Urban VIII met with Galileo and recommended he publish arguments for and against his new theory, laying out a balanced case. Instead, Galileo marched forward arrogantly, teaching his new theory as if it were already a proven fact, even before he had supporting evidence.

Then, to make matters worse, Galileo wrote a book containing a fictitious dialogue to promote his new theory which poked fun at the pope. It featured a character named Simplicio, who voiced the pope's arguments. "Simplicio" means "simpleton" or "dummy," so you can imagine how well that went over with leaders of the Church.

Finally, Galileo demanded that in light of his new theory, the Church should reinterpret the scriptures according to his findings. It's not necessarily wrong to allow modern science to illuminate the reading of the Bible, but many scientists and churchmen were shocked by Galileo's arrogance as he seemingly appointed himself a religious authority higher than even the pope.

As a result of the whole situation, the Church had Galileo tried for heresy. It's important to note that he was not being judged merely for his scientific theory but for his new and unorthodox interpretations of the scriptures that Galileo thought flowed from his theory. After Galileo was found guilty of these heretical beliefs, he was sentenced to house arrest.

Now, we should be very clear that the Church almost certainly overreacted. This was a bad decision. However, this was house arrest, not imprisonment. Galileo was given a spacious multi-room suite and was even assigned a servant to attend to him until he died of old age. Contrary to popular belief, he was never tortured; he was not shackled for years in a dungeon or dark prison cell. He lived out his days in comfort.

In the end, the Church was wise to counsel Galileo to slow down and not to promote his theory as though it had already been proven. We know today that Galileo's original theory was, in fact, wrong because he believed the planets orbited the sun in a perfect circle, whereas they actually have an elliptical orbit.

So, in the end, both sides were right in some ways and wrong in some ways. Galileo was right to press forward in the pursuit of science and to propose heliocentrism, but he was wrong to prematurely overstate the theory as truth and to put his biblical views above the pope and other Church leaders. On the other hand, the Church was right to urge caution with Galileo's scientific findings, but it overreacted by punishing him too harshly.

Prompted by this reasoning, in 1992, under the leadership of St. John Paul II, the Catholic Church officially apologized for any injustices done to Galileo. The pope called the whole episode "a sad misunderstanding."

Fr. George Coyne, who led the Vatican's astronomical observatory, said the affair was "tragic, beyond the control of any one party." He noted that it took place at the height of the Church's battle with Protestantism, "and here was a scientist saying he interpreted scripture better than they did," which obviously ruffled many feathers. But, as Fr. Coyne confirmed, the trials were not a confrontation between science and faith, because "Galileo never presented his science to the Inquisition (the official court that tried him). Science wasn't even at the trial."

What do we make of all this? Well, the next time someone tells you that the Galileo affair proves the Church and science are at odds, you can correct that myth and explain the full story.

Let's recap the key points.

- First, Galileo's heliocentric theory wasn't new. The Church was already familiar with it, thanks to Copernicus.
- Second, the Church's caution was in line with the scientific consensus of the time. Most scientists initially rejected Galileo's proposal on scientific grounds.
- Third, the Church didn't condemn Galileo's theory, it only urged caution.
- Fourth, Galileo was tried for his heretical views toward the scriptures, not for his science.

- Fifth, he was not tortured or imprisoned but was given house arrest in a comfortable apartment along with a servant.

- Finally, the Church has since apologized for any injustices toward Galileo.

EVOLUTION

After the Galileo affair, evolution is another big reason why people conclude that faith and science are in conflict. You are probably familiar with the debates about evolution, creationism, and intelligent design. A never-ending fight rages between religious people who are skeptical about evolution and skeptics convinced that evolution is the deathblow to religion. Let's consider a few key things you need to know about this topic to talk confidently about it with friends and family.

First, the word "evolution" can mean different things to different people, so we need to be more precise. Evolution is the process by which living things develop and diversify. It's a religiously neutral word that has nothing to do with God, and it doesn't presume or even imply atheism.

Another relevant term is "evolution by natural selection." This is a specific type of evolution, and it was the great discovery of Charles Darwin. Darwin concluded that the diversity of life in our world arose through a series of small adaptations, which nature has "selected" or preserved over time. According to Darwin, in every species, small variations occur in each new offspring—longer beaks, thicker feathers, curved leaves, webbed feet, and so on. Whichever adaptations make it easier for that species to survive usually remain, while those that make it harder for the species to survive are usually filtered out over a long period of time.

When Darwin proposed this theory in 1859, it made many religious people nervous. Some interpreted the theory to mean God didn't directly create every distinct species, as a literal reading of Genesis might seem to imply. Instead, God would have created a relatively small number of species that, over time, adapted, changed, and evolved into the vast diversity of species we see today.

Like evolution in general, however, the theory of "evolution by natural selection" is religiously neutral. It's perfectly reasonable to hold that God is responsible for the diversity of species but that "evolution by natural selection" was the chosen mechanism he used. So, we can say both that God is the creator of everything and that evolution by natural selection is true. There's no contradiction.

From there, you don't need to get bogged down in all the details about evolution or the various theories in order to effectively discuss it. As a Catholic, you only need to know a few key points to be able to handle this topic well.

First, the Catholic Church doesn't teach that Genesis must be read as a literal historical account (see Myth 2 earlier in this chapter). Catholics are not obligated to believe that the cosmos was created in six literal days or that God directly created every single individual species at the beginning of the world. A long Catholic tradition going back to Augustine interprets Genesis as teaching real truths, such as God's creation of the world, but using figurative, poetic language.

Second, evolution is mainly a problem for fundamentalist Protestants—not Catholics. Because they read the entire Bible literally, they run into problems with the findings of modern science that don't support their interpretation of the scriptures. So, it's important you distinguish Catholic belief from fundamentalist Protestant views. When someone tries to tell you faith and science are in conflict because of evolution, tell them that this might be true for some religious traditions that read Genesis in a literalistic way, but as a Catholic, evolution is not a threat to your faith.

Third, the question of evolution is primarily scientific, not religious. Keep affirming this in conversation. Because Catholics have no problem with evolution, we're in the comfortable position of deferring to modern science on the question of whether to accept any particular theory. We can accept or reject a theory of evolution based on its scientific support, not on religion. Be wary of people who try to frame evolution as a religious question and not a scientific one. St. John Paul II praised evolutionary theory as "more than a hypothesis" and said the latest research "constitutes a significant argument in its favor." Pope Benedict XVI led a conference celebrating the 150th anniversary of Charles Darwin's book *On the Origin of Species*, and the conference generally confirmed the lack of conflict between evolution and Catholicism. And Pope Francis has said, "Evolution . . . is not inconsistent with the notion of creation." If evolution and Catholicism are in conflict, the last three popes certainly didn't get the message.

Finally, the only thing Catholics must believe when it comes to human origin is that the *human soul* is not a product of evolution. For details about this, read Pope Pius XII's 1951 encyclical titled *Humani Generis*.[4] The pope confirms that Catholics can follow science on the question of how different material elements have evolved over time—from our human bodies to different species to variations of plants and animals. But the soul is different. The soul did not and cannot evolve since it's an immaterial reality. God gives us the soul directly at the moment our life begins. It does not emerge or evolve from pre-existing matter.

Just to recap:

- The Catholic Church does not teach that Genesis must be read as a literal historical account.
- Evolution is mainly a problem for fundamentalist Protestants, not Catholics.
- The question of evolution is primarily scientific, not religious.
- The last three popes have spoken positively about evolution.
- The only thing that Catholics must believe is that the human soul is not a product of evolution.

TALKING TIPS AND STRATEGIES

Let's tie up all the issues we discussed with tested talking tips and strategies.

Tip 1: Separate Catholicism from fundamentalist Protestantism.

Most skeptics who contend that faith and science conflict actually mean that fundamentalist Protestantism is at odds with science, but Catholics are not fundamentalist Protestants. Catholicism does not interpret Genesis literally and does not hold to six-day creationism. It affirms that the true findings of science can never contradict the true teachings of faith. For these reasons, distinguishing between your Catholic beliefs and those of fundamentalist Protestants will solve 90 percent of the tension in conversations about faith and science.

Tip 2: Make the skeptic carry the burden of proof.

If someone says that faith and science are in conflict, kindly ask them to provide specific examples. For instance, ask them to tell you which scientific finding or theory conflicts with which specific religious teaching. From my experience, in the majority of cases the other person will mention Galileo or evolution. So, get clear and confident on both those topics and you will be able to handle most discussions.

Tip 3: Focus on the Catholic scientists.

When someone tells you that religion is anti-science, ask them if they're familiar with the impressive range of religious scientists, which include many fathers and mothers of modern science. Be prepared to name a few of the most prominent Catholic scientists, such as the ones we met in this chapter: Fr. Georges Lemaître, the formulator of the Big Bang theory; Fr. Gregor Mendel, the father of modern genetics; or Roger Bacon, the founder of the scientific method, who was also a Franciscan friar.

In their very persons these scientists debunk the idea of the conflict between faith and science. Their faith compelled them to do their scientific work because they believed that every new discovery uncovered something new about God's handiwork, and thus about God.

Tip 4: Show how science depends on Christianity.

Science has its roots in Christianity, not in the ancient advanced civilizations of Greece, Rome, Egypt, China, or India. None of these cultures produced anything like modern science. Other religions, such as Buddhism, believe the world is just an illusion, while some forms of atheism believe it's ultimately meaningless. None of these worldviews provide the right soil for science to take root.

Many mainstream historians have recognized that science arose only in Christian medieval Europe because that culture affirmed that the world was intelligible. Christianity holds that God created the world and marked it with his intelligence and order. He imbued it with reason so that we can understand it, which gives the foundation for science (see the expert interview with Dr. Stacy Trasancos that appears earlier in this chapter for more on this point).

Tip 5: Highlight areas where Catholics agree with science, even while the mainstream culture does not.

There are two main areas here where Christians embrace the findings of science while secularists mostly reject them: abortion and transgenderism. If someone says religion conflicts with modern science, mention these two cases.

First, the abortion issue. On the question of when life begins, the science is emphatically clear that a new, unique human life begins at the moment of conception. Catholics joyously agree with modern biology on this fact. It's pro-choice people who deny the clear determinations of science.

A second example is transgenderism. Science tells us there are only two biological sexes, male and female. And our genes determine which of those two sexes we are. If we have a Y chromosome, we're a male. If not, we're a female. Transgenderism advocates disagree with these views, but when they do, they're forced to deny science.

With these five talking points you will be well equipped to handle any conversation about the conflict between faith and science.

RECOMMENDED BOOKS
(in order of importance)

Trent Horn, *20 Answers: Faith and Science* (Catholic Answers Press, 2014).

In this clearly written and substantial booklet, Trent deals with the fundamental issues about faith and science. He includes questions of bioethics, stem cell research, fertility treatments, and contraception. It's an excellent follow-up to this chapter.

Stephen M. Barr, *Modern Physics and Ancient Faith* (University of Notre Dame Press, 2003).

Dr. Barr is a Catholic scientist and professor of physics who writes clearly and accessibly about cutting-edge scientific issues. Instead of dealing with historical topics like the Galileo affair, he focuses on modern questions of science, such as the origin of the universe and quantum mechanics. In this very readable book, Barr shows how the latest findings of modern physics not only fail to undermine Christianity, but actually confirm many core Christian beliefs.

Stacy A. Trasancos, *Science Was Born of Christianity: The Teaching of Fr. Stanley L. Jaki* (Habitation of Chimham Publishing, 2014).

Fr. Jaki was a Benedictine priest, theologian, distinguished scientist, and author of more than fifty books. He's someone who clearly understood the issues around faith and science. His main contribution was demonstrating that Christianity was responsible for launching the scientific revolution. In this book, Dr. Stacy Trasancos summarizes his work to show how science cannot be in conflict with religion since the Christian worldview gave birth to science itself.

Stacy A. Trasancos, *Particles of Faith: A Catholic Guide to Navigating Science* (Ave Maria Press, 2016).

In an easy-to-read style, Dr. Trasancos traces the history of the conflict between faith and science and considers the main issues in the physical and biological sciences. If I could give someone just one all-in-one book that considers science from a Catholic point of view, this is the one I would offer.

Christopher T. Baglow, *Faith, Science, and Reason: Theology on the Cutting Edge* (Midwest Theological Forum, 2009).

Written especially for high school students, this vivid and engaging book explains all the relevant issues at a level that will appeal to teenagers. This is a perfect book for parents to read with their teens as a supplement to their science and religion courses. Conversations about the book will help them understand that science and faith are not in conflict.

FOR REFLECTION AND DISCUSSION

1. What was the Enlightenment and how did it contribute to the rise of the conflict between faith and science?
2. What does the Catholic Church teach about faith and science?
3. What is scientism? What do you think is the best way to persuade someone that it is a false point of view?
4. Explain how Christianity made science possible.
5. Do you think the Church was fair or harsh in dealing with Galileo?
6. Explain the reasons why evolution is not a problem for Catholics.

FOR PRACTICE

For each of the following scenarios, write a response using what you learned in this chapter.

1. Dr. Jerry Coyne, an atheist, says, "My argument is not that religious people are constantly battling science or trying to prevent it moving forward, but that the methods that religion uses to ascertain truths about the universe are at odds with the methods that science uses. They're in competition with each other. Theologians will admit this unless they're dissimulating. Religion doesn't have a reliable way to discern truth and this is the real conflict. It's a conflict of

methodology, it's a conflict of philosophy, and ultimately, it's a conflict of outcomes."

2. A friend says, "The Catholic Church is obviously
   against science and progress. They opposed Galileo,
   and they opposed Darwin. They still want to prevent
   gays from getting married and want to force women
   to have children. The Church is a despicable institu-
   tion if you ask me."

JESUS' RESURRECTION

In 132 BC, a man named Simon bar Kokhba led a revolution in Israel. Many Jews claimed that he was the Messiah, the hero who would restore Israel and conquer its enemies. He performed many signs, wonders, and miracles, and he fulfilled many of the messianic prophecies. His followers even minted coins that said, "Year One of Bar Kokhba." In other words, they were so convinced he was the Chosen One of God that they reoriented their calendars to coincide with the year that bar Kokhba was born. Does that sound familiar?

As we might expect, the Romans were not happy about any of this. They staged a massive campaign to crush bar Kokhba and his revolution, a battle that took three years. Eventually, the Romans stopped the revolution and executed bar Kokhba. And today, few people remember bar Kokhba or think he is the savior of the world. His death was the end of the story; no one worships a dead man.

Now, compare the story of bar Kokhba with the story of Jesus of Nazareth. Like bar Kokhba, Jesus was a revolutionary. He performed many signs, wonders, and miracles. His followers were convinced he was the one to vanquish Israel's enemies. And like bar Kokhba, the Romans brutally executed him.

Yet we still talk about Jesus today. Why? The simple answer is the Resurrection. What sets Jesus apart from every false messiah or religious founder is the stunning fact that he rose from the dead. The Resurrection is the foundation of Christianity. It is the Good News around which everything else revolves.

Today, however, many people question the Resurrection. Most people do not believe that Jesus rose from the dead. If a close friend or family member challenged you and said, "How could you possibly believe in the Resurrection? Do you have any evidence to show that Jesus rose from the dead?" If you're like most Christians, you wouldn't know what to say. You *believe* that Jesus rose from the dead, but you don't know how to explain that belief.

But if that's you, don't worry, because this chapter will show you how to convince others that the Resurrection really happened.

You will learn

- why the Resurrection matters;
- how to make the case for the Resurrection;
- ways to refute alternative theories about the Resurrection; and
- how to answer the best objections to the Resurrection.

To prepare yourself to get the most out of the chapter, I strongly recommend that before you begin, you first get out your Bible and read the last two chapters in each of the four gospels. Those eight chapters give an account of Jesus'

Crucifixion and the Resurrection (Matthew 27 and 28, Mark 15 and 16, Luke 23 and 24, and John 20 and 21). Reading those biblical chapters first will make everything in this chapter easier to understand.

WHY THE RESURRECTION MATTERS

As a college student, if you had asked me whether I believed in the Resurrection, I probably would have said yes. But I would have meant that in the same way that I *believed* in democracy or *believed* in Martin Luther King Jr. It would have been a simple affirmation that the Resurrection was a powerful, meaningful event that brings hope and joy to many people. I affirmed it.

But once I began questioning my own beliefs and studying the roots of Christianity, I was forced to ask myself, "Jesus' Resurrection may be inspiring, but did it really happen? Is it a historical fact? Is it true?" For Christianity, this is the pivotal question: did Jesus rise from the dead? If yes, then Christianity is true, and Jesus is God. If no, then Christianity is false, and Jesus is, at best, just one interesting teacher among many.

St. Paul articulated the stakes well. In his first letter to the Corinthians he said, "If Christ has not been raised, then our preaching is vain and your faith is in vain" (1 Cor 15:14). He couldn't be plainer. If Jesus did not rise from the dead, we're all fools and should give up Christianity.

In fact, when we talk about the Gospel, or the Good News, we're speaking primarily about the Resurrection.

Peter Kreeft, the popular Catholic philosopher, points out
that:

> The Gospel is the good news of Christ's Resurrec-
> tion. The message that set hearts on fire, changed
> lives, and turned the world upside down was not
> "love your neighbor." Every morally sane person
> already knew that; it was not news. The news was
> that a man who claimed to be the Son of God and
> the Savior of the world had risen from the dead.[1]

Along those same lines, Bishop Robert Barron says:

> When the first Christians proclaimed the Gospel,
> they didn't say a word about Jesus' preaching;
> what they talked about was his Resurrection from
> the dead. Look through all of Paul's letters, and
> you'll find a few words about Jesus' "philoso-
> phy," but you'll find, constantly, almost obses-
> sively, reiterated the claim that God raised Jesus
> from death.[2]

That leads to a natural question: why do we believe that
God raised Jesus from death? Christians give many answers
to this question. Some believe it purely through personal
intuition or experience. They may say, as the old hymn
goes, "You ask me how I know he lives? He lives within
my heart!" Although this answer may suffice at the personal
level, it is subjective and unlikely to convince anyone else.
Such a person might really be experiencing the risen Jesus
. . . or perhaps they're just deluded. We don't know.

If we're hoping to talk about the Resurrection with friends and family and persuade them that Jesus really rose from the dead, what we need is *objective* evidence of the Resurrection, evidence that is independent of our own personal feelings or experience.

This is part of what sets Christianity apart from many other religions, that because it is rooted in history, it can be investigated objectively. We have an extraordinary amount of historical testimony surrounding the life and death of Jesus, including four independent biographies containing eyewitness accounts. We also have numerous historical references outside the Bible. That's where the evidence lies, and that's what we're going to explore in this chapter.

We're going to make two major assumptions. First, we're going to assume God exists. For if God doesn't exist, then there would be no miracles and thus no Resurrection. Jesus would be just a man, and his apparent rising from the dead must have had some other natural explanation. (If the person you're talking with doubts that God exists, I encourage you to pick up the first volume of *What to Say and How to Say It*, which teaches you how to convince atheists of this basic fact.)

The second assumption is that the major historical facts about Jesus found in the New Testament are reliable. (Once again, see the previous *What to Say and How to Say It*, which makes this case in great detail.) This doesn't necessarily assume the four gospels are accurate in every little detail—although we Catholics do believe the Bible is

inerrant—it only means that, at a minimum, the basic testi-
monies recorded about Jesus' death, burial, and postmortem
appearances are trustworthy as historical accounts or at
least as trustworthy as other historical texts from the ancient
world. To prove the Resurrection, we need facts rooted in
history, and that's what the gospels provide.

THREE CRUCIAL HISTORICAL FACTS

When I began to study the Resurrection, I was told that
while many Christians believed that Jesus rose from the
dead, few professional scholars took that view seriously. But
after a little research, I was stunned to learn that a surge of
new scholarship has provided more scholarly support for
the Resurrection than at any other point in history.

One of the most interesting contributions to this fresh
wave is the "minimal facts" approach to demonstrating
the Resurrection. It was pioneered by two Evangelicals:
historian and theologian Gary Habermas and apologist
William Lane Craig. This simple method is the best way to
show someone quickly and easily the truth of the Resurrection. Let's learn that strategy, so you can use it in your
conversations.

The minimal facts approach involves two steps. First,
we look at a small number of historical facts that virtually
everyone agrees on. This consensus includes not only Christian scholars but even atheist and agnostic experts. Second,
we consider the best explanation for those facts.

Philosophers call this type of analysis "inductive reasoning." This inquiry starts from a few known facts and then ponders the best possible explanation. This is the main approach used by scientists. You also see this in most criminal court cases, where the facts are laid on the table and the jury has to decide the best explanation for them.

So, let's start with the facts. Almost all historians recognize the fact that Jesus of Nazareth was crucified and killed by Roman leaders in Jerusalem about 2,000 years ago. Once again, this is affirmed not only by religious scholars but even most atheist historians. They also agree on three widely accepted facts concerning what happened *after* Jesus' death:

1. **The empty tomb:** A few days after being crucified and buried, Jesus' tomb was discovered empty.
2. **The postmortem appearances:** After Jesus' death, hundreds of people claimed to have encountered him, including skeptics and enemies.
3. **The origin of Christianity:** Suddenly, in the middle of the first century, a new religion (Christianity) sprung up among the most devout followers of another religion (Judaism).

Before getting into the best explanation for those facts, let's look at them one at a time to see why virtually all scholars agree about them.

The Empty Tomb

How do we know Jesus' tomb was discovered empty? William Lane Craig offers five independent lines of evidence supporting this fact. Let's consider a few of them.

The first are the early eyewitness accounts. We have six independent accounts of Jesus' burial and empty tomb. At least two—a passage quoted in the Gospel of Mark and another quoted by Paul in 1 Corinthians 15—scholars date back to within just five to ten years of Jesus' death. Historians generally celebrate when they locate *two* independent accounts of the same event. The fact that we have *six* early, independent accounts confirming the empty tomb gives us extraordinary confidence.

Another reason to believe the tomb was found empty is the simplicity of Mark's account, widely believed to be the earliest. His story lacks any sign of legendary development and is not embellished with theological motifs.

A third reason involves the women who discovered the empty tomb. Women were not regarded as credible witnesses in first-century Jewish society, and their testimony was not admitted in court. If you were an ancient Jew, inventing a story about people discovering an empty tomb, why make the witnesses women? Surely, if the empty tomb story were a legend, the principle witnesses would have been male disciples. That women appear first at the tomb, consistently in all the accounts, suggests that the writers—no matter how embarrassed they were by this fact—recorded that women discovered the empty tomb because that's the way it happened.

Finally, a fourth line of support is the early attempt of Jewish authorities to disprove the empty tomb. Matthew tells us that the religious leaders fabricated a story, accusing Jesus' disciples of stealing Jesus' body. But this would only make sense if the tomb were, in fact, empty! So, the early Jewish adversaries provide more evidence for belief in the empty tomb.

The Postmortem Appearances

Let's turn to the second fact—the appearances of Jesus after his death. Once again, we have multiple, independent accounts that give us great confidence in this fact. The primary record is found in Paul's first letter to the Corinthians:

> For I handed on to you as of first importance what I also received: that Christ died for our sins in accordance with the scriptures; that he was buried; that he was raised on the third day in accordance with the scriptures; that he appeared to Cephas, then to the Twelve. After that, he appeared to more than five hundred brothers at once, most of whom are still living, though some have fallen asleep. After that he appeared to James, then to all the apostles. Last of all, as to one born abnormally, he appeared to me. (1 Cor 15:3–8)

Scholars date this passage to within five to ten years of the appearances themselves. And what gives it even more credibility is Paul's declaring that "he appeared to more than five hundred brothers at once, most of whom are still living."

The implicit suggestion seems to be, "If you doubt this, go talk to the eyewitnesses who encountered the risen Jesus!" Paul would not have challenged people in this way if the event had never taken place.

The Origin of Christianity

A third well-attested fact is the sudden origin of Christianity. Everyone knows that Christianity sprang into being midway through the first century. But that raises the obvious questions: Why did it come into existence? What launched this movement?

Even skeptical scholars recognize that the Christian faith arose because something profound happened, not only among the first disciples of Jesus but also among thousands of others who embraced this new Christian way. The fact is that Christianity rapidly developed in the early first century only because the disciples sincerely believed that God had raised Jesus from the dead. They proclaimed it by their words and their deaths.

The empty tomb, the postmortem appearances, and the origin of Christianity are three solid, important facts. But as with any investigative case, the facts aren't enough. We need to determine the best explanation for those facts, and that's what we'll explore next.

HOW DO WE CHOOSE THE BEST EXPLANATION?

We have considered three historical facts about Jesus' Resurrection that almost all scholars agree on, but facts don't explain themselves. For instance, in a court case, after attorneys have presented Exhibits A, B, and C, they must show the theory that best accounts for all this evidence.

Several theories propose to explain these facts, and thus account for the Resurrection. Christians think God raised Jesus from the dead, and that best explains all the facts. But many nonbelievers hold that the disciples were just hallucinating, that they stole the body, or that Jesus never really died on the Cross in the first place. In order to determine the best theory, we must explore how historians decide among alternatives.

Historians rely on five criteria to assess different theories. You don't have to memorize these, but it's worth knowing about them in case someone accuses you of just assuming the Resurrection is true, without considering the alternative theories. With these criteria in mind, you can say, "Actually, I don't believe in the Resurrection for arbitrary reasons. I believe it because it best accounts for the evidence, and here's why . . . ."

Let's consider the five criteria that historians use to evaluate different explanations. The first criterion is explanatory scope. The best theory should explain most or all of the facts. For instance, if Explanation A only accounts for two of the facts, but Explanation B explains all three facts, then the latter would be the better option.

The second criterion is explanatory power. The best theory should account for the facts forcefully, not in a weak or cursory way. A good explanation should make you think,

"Ah! That's it!" and not, "Yeah, I guess I could see how that maybe explains the facts."

The third criterion is plausibility. The best explanation should be credible, given the existing background information. It should make sense and not make you think, "That seems very far-fetched and unlikely." For instance, if the facts we have are a broken window with a baseball-sized hole, and a group of kids playing baseball on the lawn below, a theory that suggests the kids hit a baseball through the window would be plausible. It would not be plausible, however, that a baseball player on the moon hit a mega home run that entered our atmosphere and crashed through the window.

The fourth criterion asks if the explanation is contrived. The best theory should not require adopting many new beliefs for which we have no evidence. For instance, suppose we were trying to explain the construction of the pyramids in Egypt. Some theories suggest, with archaeological evidence, that they were erected with an innovative system of ramps, levers, and pulleys. That's certainly possible. But others contrive that aliens built them, which requires not only a belief in aliens but a belief that aliens visited Earth at some point and decided to build large pyramids, none of which we have evidence for. Thus, aliens would be a contrived explanation.

The fifth and final criterion is coherence with accepted beliefs. The best explanation will conflict with the fewest accepted beliefs. We have many accepted beliefs, such as the laws of physics to the facts of history. The best explanation usually aligns with them. If a theory forces us to overturn the law of gravity or the fact that Abraham Lincoln was president of the United States, that's a huge strike against it.

To sum all this up, when comparing different explanations, the best theory explains the full scope of facts, has more explanatory power, is most plausible, is not contrived, and is in line with accepted beliefs.

What does all this have to do with the Resurrection? Well, as we've seen, we have three facts that have tremendous support: the empty tomb, the postmortem appearances, and the origin of Christianity. We also have a number of possible explanations for those facts, including the Resurrection, hallucinations, stolen bodies, and more. So, next we will use these criteria to consider which explanation is best.

EXAMINING THE ALTERNATIVE THEORIES

In this chapter, we will consider five prominent theories about the Resurrection and use the historians' criteria to determine which one makes the most sense. If you get familiar with these five, you can be confident the next time you talk with a Resurrection skeptic.

We'll save the Christian theory until the end, the theory that Jesus actually rose from the dead. We'll start with four naturalistic theories skeptics put forward—explanations with no supernatural or miraculous involvement—and determine if any of them can possibly work. If all four come up short, that will leave only one plausible option—that God raised Jesus from the dead.

The Conspiracy Theory

The first theory is the Conspiracy Theory. This one holds that the disciples stole Jesus' body and lied about his appearances, making the Resurrection a complete hoax. Notably, this counter-explanation is mentioned in the Gospel of Matthew as the Jewish leaders' cover-up for the discomforting fact of the empty tomb. It also became a very popular theory in the eighteenth century.

However, the Conspiracy Theory has been almost completely abandoned today by historians because it doesn't hold up when judged by all five criteria. It does do well on explanatory scope, because it explains all three facts (the tomb was empty because Jesus' body was stolen, the postmortem appearances were really lies fabricated by the disciples, and Christianity arose because the disciples just made it all up). But it fails to meet the other criteria.

First, it lacks explanatory power. Why would the disciples make up a story about women discovering the empty tomb? And how could they have taken a body from a stone tomb, guarded by Roman soldiers? Also, as scholars have recognized, there is no evidence the disciples were lying, and plenty of evidence that they were truthful. Even skeptics acknowledge that the earliest disciples sincerely believed that God had raised Jesus from the dead, and that they were willing to die to testify to that belief. People die for false beliefs all the time, such as terrorists flying planes into buildings because they think it's God's will. But no one dies for a belief they *know* is false.

Also, the Conspiracy Theory seems contrived. It requires us to doubt every event and bit of testimony recorded by multiple, independent sources.

For these reasons and more, no serious scholar today defends the Conspiracy Theory. The only place you read about it is in the dark corners of atheist websites or in the sensationalist press.

The Apparent Death Theory

A second widespread alternative is the Apparent Death Theory. This one suggests that when Jesus was taken down from the Cross, he wasn't really dead but merely unconscious. He was then revived in the tomb and somehow escaped to convince his disciples he had risen from the dead.

Muslims believe this explanation. In fact, the Quran says that "they slew him not, it only appeared so." Some Muslim scholars interpret that to mean Jesus only seemed to die but actually fainted on the Cross. Other Muslim scholars suggest Jesus had a secret twin brother who was crucified in his place.

The Apparent Death Theory was somewhat popular in the nineteenth century, when many people held to a version known as the Swoon Theory, but this opinion has almost no supporters today because it doesn't explain our three facts.

First, the theory fails the test of plausibility. It's not credible that anyone, much less a man who had been tortured and beaten to the brink of death, could survive a Roman crucifixion. The Romans were experts at killing people. Ancient records show that if a centurion failed to execute a condemned criminal or botched a crucifixion, the centurion's punishment would be death. This explains why centurions often broke the victim's legs and speared them—both were ways to be doubly sure the victim had died.

Moreover, the theory is contrived. It stretches the imagination to think that even if Jesus survived the blood bath of his Crucifixion, he could somehow escape from his tomb that was sealed by a huge stone and then convince people that he was the Lord of life who had gloriously conquered death.

Thus, the Apparent Death Theory is implausible, extremely contrived, and goes against the accepted beliefs about what medicine and biology tell us about bodies that have been scourged and crucified. For these reasons, the Apparent Death Theory has virtually no defenders today among New Testament historians.

The Displaced Body Theory

The Displaced Body Theory suggests that Joseph of Arimathea placed Jesus' body in his family's tomb, but only temporarily, later moving it to the common graveyard reserved for criminals. Unaware that the corpse had been moved, the disciples found the tomb empty and believed that Jesus had been raised from the dead.

The big problem with this theory is its limited explanatory scope—it doesn't explain all the facts. It accounts for the empty tomb, but not the postmortem appearances of Jesus.

Second, it has weak explanatory power. If Joseph of Arimathea and his helpers moved the body, why didn't they correct the disciples when the disciples proclaimed that Jesus rose from the dead? We have no record of such a correction, not even from Jesus' enemies, who would have been glad to debunk the disciples' claims.

We also know from Jewish records that the criminal graveyard in Jerusalem was fewer than 600 yards from the site of Jesus' Crucifixion. If Joseph planned to move Jesus' corpse there eventually, he would have just done it immediately. This makes the theory very contrived, as does ascribing motives and activities to Joseph of Arimathea for which we have no evidence.

Thus, like the other theories, this one has little support among historians. Only a few amateur bloggers and online atheists take it seriously.

The Hallucination Theory

The Hallucination Theory is probably the most fashionable naturalistic alternative to the Resurrection, the one that most skeptics adopt. It claims the Resurrection appearances were merely hallucinations among the disciples. Despite hundreds of people thinking that they had encountered Jesus, they were really all deluded.

This view has several problems. First, it has poor explanatory scope. Most notably, it says nothing about the empty tomb. This theory forces you to add another explanation, such as the Conspiracy Theory, to account for the fact that Jesus' body was gone.

Second, it fails to explain the origin of Christianity and the disciples' sudden conviction that Jesus had risen from the dead. In the first century, as today, people sometimes saw visions of their loved ones after their death. However, then as today, people didn't interpret these visions to mean that the person had somehow risen from the dead. As the prominent biblical scholar N. T. Wright has observed, visions of deceased persons were not taken as evidence that they are alive but as evidence that they were dead!

Even if the disciples were merely seeing ethereal visions of Jesus, they would not automatically take those as proof that Jesus had physically risen from the dead and returned to this world. What convinced them of that fact was the bodily nature of his Resurrection. They could feel and touch Jesus, eat with him, and experience his glorified body. Yet none of that is accounted for by the Hallucination Theory.

More problems discredit this theory, but I'll briefly mention just two: it defies both the coherence with accepted beliefs and plausibility. Regarding the former criterion, modern psychology accepts the conclusion that hallucinations are not a group phenomenon. It may be plausible that one person could have had such a hallucination, or perhaps even two or three, but hundreds of people experiencing the same hallucination in all different contexts defies known science, and thus it is highly implausible.

The Hallucination Theory has outlived its rival theories and is the most popular option among non-Christians today. But the crucial question is whether it outstrips the fifth and final theory, the Resurrection.

The Resurrection Theory

The Resurrection Theory says what the historical texts claim: that Jesus was crucified and died, that he was buried in a tomb, but that God then raised him bodily from the dead.

How does this theory fare by the historians' criteria? It has the best explanatory scope. It supports all three facts—the empty tomb, the postmortem appearances, and the origin of Christianity—whereas the rival explanations only attempt to explain one or perhaps two.

The Resurrection Theory also exhibits tremendous explanatory power, which might be its greatest virtue. This explanation forcefully shows it is reasonable that the tomb should be empty, the disciples should see appearances of Jesus alive, and they should come to believe in his rising from the dead.

The Resurrection Theory also manifests high plausibility once we accept the premises that God exists and that the accounts of Jesus found in the New Testament are reliable.

The Resurrection Theory is not contrived, because it requires no new suppositions. The other hypotheses all require many more new assumptions, such as that the disciples were all liars or deluded or that the Roman soldiers really didn't kill Jesus.

Finally, the Resurrection Theory coheres with accepted beliefs. That is, the theory is not disputed by commonly held convictions. Someone might object that it contradicts the accepted belief that people don't rise from the dead, but this isn't a real contradiction because we can believe both that dead people don't naturally rise from the dead and that God supernaturally raised Jesus from the dead. There's no conflict there. We agree that without supernatural aid, dead people stay dead. But Christians don't argue that Jesus rose from the dead *naturally* or by his own effort. We assert that God the Father raised Jesus from the dead by a *supernatural* act.

So, where do we stand? We've seen how the four naturalistic theories—the Conspiracy Theory, the Apparent Death Theory, the Displaced Body Theory, and the Hallucination Theory—all have devastating flaws and fail to account for all the evidence. We've also seen how the Resurrection Theory fares astonishingly well. It accounts for all the facts, requires no contrived new beliefs, and seems very plausible given that God exists, and Jesus prophesied his own Resurrection (which we didn't have space to cover here).

All this means that we can know from a fair, historical analysis—just as historians analyze any other event in ancient history—that God did in fact raise Jesus from the dead. Anyone who doubts that claim must do one of two things: they must either suggest a more plausible theory than the Resurrection Theory, or they must refute the Resurrection Theory and show why it's false.

We've already defused that first option, showing how even the best alternatives come up short. But next we'll look at how some skeptics pursue the second option, trying to debunk the Resurrection Theory.

Expert Interview with Carl Olson

➤ **Watch the interview here: https://claritasu.com/olson**

Carl Olson is editor of Catholic World Report and Ignatius Insight. He is the author of several books, including *Did Jesus Really Rise from the Dead?: Questions and Answers about the Life, Death, and Resurrection*, which I think is the best Catholic book on the topic that we're exploring here.

In this interview, Carl responds to the following questions:

1. Why is the Resurrection important?
2. Is there any evidence that the stories about Jesus' Resurrection were just cobbled together from other religions or ancient pagan myths?
3. Would it be more difficult to explain Christianity without the Resurrection than to defend the Resurrection?
4. What do you think of the claim that historical sciences are simply not helpful when it comes to the question of a miracle like the Resurrection?
5. What does St. Paul offer on the topic of the Resurrection?
6. What would you say is the best objection to the Resurrection of Jesus from the dead, and how would you respond to it?
7. What are a few tips or principles that Catholics should keep in mind whenever discussing the Resurrection with a skeptic?

Excerpt from the Interview

"What we have is this master, this rabbi who is suddenly arrested. He's crucified. He's put in a tomb. And his followers are scared. They're frightened. They're scattered, except for, of course, the few women and John who go to the Cross. Then suddenly a few weeks later they're out there preaching, saying, 'We believe in this man, Jesus Christ, that he was sent by God, that he was crucified by the Jewish leaders and the Romans and so forth, and that he has been resurrected.' What you find again and again, not just in Acts 2, but throughout the writings of Peter, Paul, and others, is the central theme is not 'God wants us to be good people' or that 'Jesus is a nice example,' but that Jesus rose from the dead." (Carl Olson)

ANSWERING THE BEST OBJECTIONS

There are many people who doubt the Resurrection. Do a random polling of your friends and family and ask them, "Do you think Jesus rose from the dead?" You'll get some yeses but also a lot of nos. Why do people still have such doubts? Let's look at four of the most common objections you'll hear from skeptics, and you'll learn how to answer each of them.

Objection 1: "The stories of Jesus' Resurrection are just recycled versions of pagan myths about dying and rising gods."

The view that the biblical Jesus is not a historical person and that he never existed is known as "mythicism." Richard Dawkins, probably the world's most famous atheist, has flirted with this opinion in his books, and you'll find it heavily represented among YouTube videos and atheist blogs. Mythicists suggest that Jesus was not a real person but that the stories about him were just cobbled together from various pagan myths.

But about this notion, C. S. Lewis, an expert in ancient mythology, said that anyone who claims Jesus was a myth has not read many myths. To respond to this view, you should do two things. First, ask the skeptic which specific myth or which mythical figure the story of Jesus parallels. If they can't point to specifics, it's a sign that they're just regurgitating something they've heard online or read in a book but for which they have no support. In fact, there are no direct mythical equivalents for the Resurrection of Jesus. It's an unprecedented event in human history.

We do have stories of mythical gods being assumed into heaven (such as Hercules and Romulus). Some legends tell of heroes disappearing into a higher realm (such as Apollonius and Empedocles). We have examples of gods such as Osiris and Adonis that represent seasonal symbols for the crop cycle, dying in the dry season and coming back to life in the rainy season, but even these latter cases are nothing like the Christian concept of resurrection.

In the most commonly suggested equivalent, Osiris was murdered, dismembered, and scattered around the world. Later, his body parts were recovered and rejoined, and he was rejuvenated. Osiris then journeyed to the underworld, where he became the lord of the dead. He did not resurrect with a glorified body and walk with people on earth, as Jesus did. He was not alive again as was Jesus but was instead a dead god who never returned among the living.

In every case, the comparisons between Jesus and pagan gods are spurious at best, as the mythical gods share little in common with Jesus. Pagan myths are not rooted in history; Jesus' Resurrection is.

Objection 2: "There are too many discrepancies in the Resurrection accounts to take them seriously."

Even if it were true that the gospels contained minor inconsistencies that cannot be reconciled, that doesn't discount the truths affirmed independently by all the sources. (Though again, we Catholics *do* believe any inconsistencies can be reconciled. For the sake of argument, however, we'll assume they cannot.)

For example, the gospel accounts about the empty tomb seem to differ in minor ways. One gospel says Mary Magdalene was first to discover the empty tomb, while another gospel says a different Mary joined her, and a third gospel says that Simon and another disciple came to the tomb.

Similarly, one gospel account mentions two angels at the empty tomb, and another mentions only one. But even if the stories were in conflict over these minor details, all the gospels consistently agree that the tomb *was discovered empty*. That's the key historical fact. Who discovered the tomb or how many angels were initially present does not change this essential fact.

Regardless of any minor discrepancies—and I emphasize that these are *apparent* inconsistencies and not *actual* contradictions—all of our sources agree on at least the three facts we have focused on here: the empty tomb, the postmortem appearances, and the sudden origin of Christianity. Multiple, independent sources confirm those realities, and they must be taken seriously even if there are minor discrepancies.

Objection 3: "The earliest gospel, the Gospel of Mark, had no Resurrection account. That was added later. How could Mark have left out this most important event?"

This objection refers to Mark chapter 16. Most of our earliest manuscripts end with verse 8, which covers the disciples finding the empty tomb and an angel announcing that Jesus had been raised. Verses 9 through 20, however, contain appearances of Jesus to the other disciples, but these verses do not appear in our earliest manuscripts.

In response to the objection you should make three observations. First, even scholars who think the last section of Mark was added later admit that the earlier chapters of the Gospel of Mark point to the Resurrection, since in chapters eight, nine, and ten Jesus predicts that he would rise from the dead. Also, even the shorter version of Mark ends with an empty tomb and an angel announcing that Jesus had been raised from the dead.

Second, you can point out that there are good reasons to think the last section of the gospel wasn't added later but was instead part of the original document yet was accidentally dropped from the earliest copies. A common theory holds that one early copy was made without the ending, and then future copies made from this manuscript did not carry it, too.

Third, and this is the more important response, you can say that the Resurrection doesn't depend only on the ending of Mark. The other three gospels affirm it, as do the letters of St. Paul, all of which are dated earlier than the Gospel of Mark.

Objection 4: "I don't believe Jesus rose from the dead because it's just impossible for that to happen. It's too far-fetched."

If critics says something like this, you have to probe a little deeper to identify the issue. Either people think that because we have no other example of someone rising from the dead, it's unlikely and hard to believe. Or they contend that miracles are altogether impossible, and in that case it's unbelievable that Jesus miraculously rose from the dead.

You can actually agree with opponents that nothing like the Resurrection has ever happened before or since. But this doesn't mean it's an impossible event. It just means that it is rare and unique, which is what Christians believe. That being said, when we account for the context of Jesus' Resurrection, including his claims to be God and his prophecies that he would rise from the dead, the Resurrection becomes far more credible.

When people deny the Resurrection because they reject the possibility of miracles, you should delicately push back. Ask them, "Why do you think miracles are impossible?" Making this claim puts forward a philosophical view that demands the support of reasons. Apply a little pressure. If skeptics think miracles are impossible, ask for evidence. Chances are high that they can't and won't defend their view. In many cases, critics base their objection on emotional resistance. Something inside them feels off about the idea of Jesus being raised from the dead. The key is to help them realize that their resistance is not based on logic or reason but on feelings, and feelings can be fickle and overcome.

These responses should give you clarity and confidence to deal with four of the main objections to the Resurrection.

TALKING TIPS AND STRATEGIES

Next, let's consider some powerful tips and strategies that will help you discuss the Resurrection more effectively with a friend or family member.

Tip 1: Do some reading.

Pick at least one book on the Resurrection and read it carefully. The Resurrection is a surprisingly complicated subject with many details to examine—multiple accounts, historical analysis, facts and counter-facts, theories, and rebuttals. If you want to be clear and confident in speaking about the Resurrection, you have to study it well. At the end of this chapter, I'll recommend the best books on the topic, but pick one and spend a little time with it.

Tip 2: Set the stakes.

When you're talking about the Resurrection, make sure your conversation partner understands its significance. If they are non-Christians, make it clear that the Resurrection is critical. If the Resurrection didn't happen, Christianity is false. If they are half-heartedly Christian but aren't quite sure what to make of the Resurrection, emphasize that they really should figure out what they believe about it, for the same reasons.

When you set the stakes in this way, you ramp up their interest. Suddenly you're not talking about some pointless, abstract issue. You're talking about the most crucial event in human history on which the world's most prominent religion either rises or falls.

Tip 3: Don't get lost in the weeds.

Don't bog down your conversation with unnecessary details. For instance, discussing whether there were one or two angels at the empty tomb distracts from the main points under consideration. Stick with the basic facts we have considered: the empty tomb, the postmortem appearances, and the sudden rise of Christianity. Keep bringing the conversation back to those facts.

Tip 4: Use the inductive approach.

Explain to the other person that perhaps it would be best to split the conversation in two. First, you can start with the facts that you both agree on, then second, you can discuss what best explains those facts. That's the same strategy we used throughout this chapter.

The benefit of this approach is that you don't have to start by making a positive case for the Resurrection Theory. Instead, once you establish the three facts, you can spend most of your time exposing the alternative naturalistic theories, showing why they fail to explain the facts.

Tip 5: Identify the point of resistance.

If the other person still doesn't accept the Resurrection, after all that, you want to identify the point of resistance. The Resurrection is a very hard thing for many people to accept. It's strange and extraordinary. So, don't be surprised when someone resists the Resurrection, despite all the evidence, and still refuses to accept it.

One approach is to openly admit that a man rising from the dead *can* seem strange. So, you can affirm that reaction, but then try to determine the specific things holding them back by asking for specific objections or criticisms. This will do one of two things: it will either reveal an objection the person is struggling with, and that will give you a chance to help overcome it, or it will show that the person doesn't have any real intellectual reasons to doubt the Resurrection but just some emotional or mental blocks. Helping them to realize this can itself be a minor victory, because your partner will be forced to admit they have no substantial objections.

Tip 6: Guide them to the next steps.

Convincing someone that the Resurrection is true is an exhilarating experience, but it's important not to stop there. When a person comes to believe in the risen Christ, you need to help them walk the next steps. You must show them the significant implications of the Resurrection. If Jesus rose from the dead, then that means Jesus is God and that he has conquered both sin and death, so neither should trouble us any longer. The Resurrection also means that Jesus is alive today, and therefore, we can interact with him here and now.

People will need time to process these implications. After they affirm the historical fact of the Resurrection, you need to guide them further in the Christian faith. The Resurrection is the doorway into Christianity, but opening that door is only the beginning, so you want to help friends and family move from the Resurrection into a relationship with the risen Jesus.

RECOMMENDED BOOKS
(in order of importance)

Carl Olson, *Did Jesus Really Rise from the Dead?: Questions and Answers about the Life, Death, and Resurrection of Jesus* (Ignatius Press, 2016).

This is the one of the best Catholic books on talking about the Resurrection. Carl condenses some of the latest scholarship into short, digestible bites. He uses a clear and accessible question-and-answer format to handle many of the popular objections.

William Lane Craig, *Did Jesus Rise from the Dead?* (Impact 360 Institute, 2019).

Craig, an Evangelical scholar and apologist, has developed a short, punchy, and easy-to-read study of the Resurrection, which I leaned on heavily for this chapter. He explores five possible theories attempting to explain the facts of the Resurrection and shows why the Resurrection Theory is the best.

Gary Habermas and Michael Licona, *The Case for the Resurrection of Jesus* (Kregel Publications, 2004).

In this apologetical classic, Evangelical scholars Habermas and Licona strike a balance between popular resources and heavier scholarly texts. This comprehensive book offers an extensive appendix containing a detailed outline of arguments and counterarguments involved in discussing the Resurrection.

William Lane Craig and Gerd Lüdemann, *Jesus Resurrection: Fact or Figment?* (IVP Academic, 2000) and *Did the Resurrection Happen?: A Conversation with Gary Habermas and Antony Flew* (IVP Books, 2009).

I recommend these two books together because they tackle the Resurrection issue not through straight didactic teaching but through debate. Craig and Habermas are Evangelical scholars, while Lüdemann is a New

Testament expert who doubts the Resurrection and Flew was a famous twentieth-century atheist.

Both books display the best cases on opposite sides of the debate. So, you get to consider not only the best Christian arguments for the Resurrection but also the best skeptical arguments against it, which will prepare you well for your conversations.

N. T. Wright, *The Resurrection of the Son of God* (Christian Origins and the Question of God, Volume 3; Fortress Press, 2003).

An Anglican bishop and New Testament scholar, Wright has written what is widely considered the magisterial book on the subject. This comprehensive and meticulous work of 740 pages will take hard work, but the effort will pay off by building your confidence in defending the Resurrection.

FOR REFLECTION AND DISCUSSION

1. What does St. Paul say about importance of the Resurrection? Why do you think his arguments are so persuasive?
2. What are the three historical facts, accepted by virtually all scholars, that concern the Resurrection? Explain the significance of each.
3. Explain why plausibility is an effective criterion for evaluating a theory of the Resurrection.

4. What is the Hallucination Theory of the Resurrection? How would you refute it?
5. What do you think is the strongest objection to the Resurrection? How would you respond to it?

FOR PRACTICE

For each of the following scenarios, write a response using what you learned in this chapter.

1. An unbeliever says, "Not all scholars accept the empty tomb as evidence of the Resurrection. One prominent scholar, John Dominic Crossan, proposes that Jesus' body was thrown in a shallow grave and perhaps eaten by dogs. So, your fact is not well established."
2. A skeptic says, "David Hume argued that we should proportion our beliefs to the evidence. Also, since a miracle is such an extraordinary claim, we would need extraordinary evidence to come to believe it. Yet Christians present no extraordinary evidence."

3

HEAVEN, HELL, AND PURGATORY

This chapter concerns some of the most important questions we can ask. Where will we spend eternity? What's our final destiny? But even though heaven, hell, and purgatory are critical concerns for us, most of us find it difficult to discuss them with family and friends.

Think about it. When was the last time you had a substantial conversation about these things? We rarely do, especially with non-Catholics, and it's often because we worry about coming across as dogmatic, or we just don't feel confident talking about heaven, hell, and purgatory. We know a little about them, but we're not sure where to draw the line between knowledge and speculation. This chapter will get you clear.

You will learn

- how to overcome resistance to discussing the Last Things: death, judgment, heaven, hell, and purgatory;

- what the Church teaches about these topics, some common misunderstandings, and how to discuss them better; and

- how to answer the best objections, such as "Heaven is a wish-fulfillment fantasy," "A good God would never send people to hell," or "Purgatory isn't in the Bible."

So, this chapter will clear things up for you and give you confidence for conversations.

WHY IT'S HARD TO TALK ABOUT THE LAST THINGS

You are probably aware that heaven, hell, and purgatory are traditionally grouped with death and judgment and collectively described as the Last Things. All three involve states of the soul and divine judgment, which is the reason why so many people get nervous talking about them.

"Judgment" is one of today's dirtiest words. How many times have you heard people say, "Don't judge" or "Don't judge me" or "Don't be so judgmental." Our culture is terrified of judgment. This is especially true for millennials and younger generations. We are reluctant to be seen as judging others. So, that explains why we avoid talking about heaven, hell, and purgatory. They are like electrical wires, and we try not to get too close to them in polite company for fear of shock.

Our culture, as you know, hyper-stresses being tolerant and nonjudgmental. We're hesitant to describe any behavior as objectively wrong, and we're wary of saying someone is going down a path that, unless they change course, will lead them to hell. After all, who are we to determine where people end up after they die?

But we should not dodge conversations about heaven and hell for they are crucial realities. Every moment of every day, we move a little closer to one of these two eternal destinies. The entire drama of our lives unfolds around this issue: whether we will finish the race and arrive in heaven or reject God and end up in hell.

How to Talk about the Last Things

So, if we want to discuss heaven, hell, and purgatory with family and friends, we must first create an environment conducive to the conversation. In my experience, it's not ideal to start with any of those three topics. Instead, the best entry point is the topic of death. A good discussion on death opens the door to speaking about the more prickly eternal topics.

But how do you do that? Aren't people just as anxious about discussing death? Well, I recommend opening the discussion with a few harmless questions. None of these judge the other person or make them feel uncomfortable. You're just raising thoughtful, interesting questions. For example, you might randomly ask in a low-key way, "Hey, I have a question for you. I've been thinking about this a lot: if you were to die right now, what would you most regret not doing before you died?" Or "Suppose you found out that you only had one month to live. What would you do differently over the next four weeks? In what ways would you change your life?"

These are simple but profound questions. They usually get people thinking about life from an eternal perspective and what, if anything, comes after death. When they say, "Well, I wish I would have done A, B, or C" or "I would probably stop doing X and start doing Y," you can reply with follow-up questions that will get them to probe even deeper. These follow-up questions will lead them to ponder what really matters at the end of life, and they will inevitably open the door to the ultimate question: "But what about *after* you die? What do you think happens then?"

That's the final door you want them to walk through because it creates an opportunity to talk about the Last Things—death, judgment, heaven, hell, and purgatory. So, I recommend that you use death as a doorway topic, asking harmless speculative questions, which will inevitably open up a conversation about eternal realities.

WHAT WE KNOW ABOUT HEAVEN

Once that happens, you can start talking directly about heaven, hell, and purgatory. It's best to start with heaven. Most people get their image of heaven from cartoons or popular art. They conceive heaven as some place floating in the clouds. It's populated by cute baby angels who lounge around, playing harps and trumpets, and singing hymns all day. But this is an unhelpful, childish conception. Frankly, if heaven were like this conception, who would want to go there? It's hardly attractive.

Descriptions of Heaven

Compare that poor caricature with St. Paul's description of heaven: "What eye has not seen, and ear has not heard, and what has not entered the human heart, God has prepared for those who love him" (1 Cor 2:9). In other words, heaven is *greater* than anything you've ever seen, *greater* than anything you've ever heard, and *greater* than the best feeling that has ever entered your heart.

St. Paul's view of heaven is similar to St. Anselm's definition of God. Anselm identifies God as "that than which nothing greater can be thought." We might describe heaven as "that eternal state of being than which nothing greater can be imagined." If you've ever felt underwhelmed by someone's depiction of heaven, take heart, for that's almost certainly not what heaven is like. On the other hand, whatever experiences, feelings, sights, or sounds have *most* filled you with joy, know that heaven is infinitely better than even those.

Another way to define heaven is to say it is where God is. It's not located in a specific spatial place, like in the clouds, as much as it's located in God himself. For this reason, Jesus often told people that "the Kingdom of Heaven is near you" or "the Kingdom of God is at hand." When you're around Jesus, you're near God (since Jesus is God in the flesh), and therefore you're already experiencing heaven.

Another way to define heaven is to say it is the fullness of communion with God. Heaven is that state where we're directly united to God, without anything separating us or mediating our relationship. The sacraments, especially the Eucharist, are often called foretastes of heaven because they establish union with God. But even so, they're just a preview, not the reality, because the union is incomplete. The sacraments still involve intermediaries, whether they're priests celebrating the sacrament or the material elements used in the sacrament. Only in heaven do we achieve full, unmediated communion with God.

Common Misunderstandings

With those helpful definitions in mind, we should next clear up a few common misunderstandings about heaven. First, heaven is not so much a place as a state of being. It's not a location within our spatial-temporal universe. In 1961, Yuri Gagarin, a Russian cosmonaut, became the first man in space. When he returned to earth, he reportedly said, "I looked and looked and looked, but I didn't see God." But that's exactly the wrong way to understand God or heaven. Heaven is not a spatial location somewhere millions of light-years away that we might discover if only we could reach far enough into the galaxy. It's not a place at all, in the spatial sense—it's a state of being.

Second, heaven does not involve sitting in clouds, playing harps, and singing hymns all day. These depictions are symbols that point to something true, but they're not meant to be taken literally. The clouds declare that heaven exists in a higher realm. The harps suggest beautiful music, that in heaven we will be enveloped by beauty and harmony. The hymns symbolize the praise of God. But none of these images mean heaven will be an eternal, boring church service. Remember, heaven is *greater* than the most wonderful things you've experienced, not less. This is important to affirm to people who feel unimpressed by or unattracted to heaven.

So, when it comes to defining heaven, the important takeaways are:

- Heaven is not a place in space, but a state of being.
- Heaven is the dwelling place of God.
- Heaven is greater than anything you have ever seen, heard, or experienced.

WHAT WE KNOW ABOUT HELL

What about the flip side? What is hell like? Art and film have portrayed hell so often that lots of images immediately come to mind. Prominently, Dante's depiction in *The Divine Comedy* leads many people to envision devils, torture, and pain. The most common depiction involves a horned devil in red pajamas, poking unrepentant sinners with a pitchfork as flames burst around them.

All these images represent *something* about hell, just as harps and clouds tell us *something* about heaven, but they are only symbols and should not be taken literally. The Catholic Church teaches that hell is not a place of fire but a state of being like heaven. Probably the simplest way to understand hell is to say that hell is the opposite of heaven. Because heaven is better than the best thing you could imagine, hell must be worse than the worst thing you could imagine.

Hell is a deprivation of eternal happiness, just as cold is a deprivation of heat or evil a deprivation of good. Hell involves missing out on the goods of heaven, including the greatest good, which is direct communion with God and all the saints.

The best definition can be found in the *Catechism of the Catholic Church (CCC)*, which teaches that "Hell is the state of definitive self-exclusion from communion with God and the blessed" (*CCC*, 1033). That's a strong but wordy definition, so let's unpack it.

First, we can tell from the first two words ("Hell is") that hell actually exists. It is not fictitious, imaginary, or symbolic. Despite an increasing number of Christians who deny the existence of hell, it is real and it's possible that people may end up there. Anyone who dies in a state of unrepentant mortal sin will end up in hell.

Second, from the *Catechism*'s definition we see hell is a "state." Hell is not a place. It's not located somewhere in our world or somewhere else in the cosmos. It is a state of being separated from God and from communion with the saints.

Third, hell is definitive. According to the *Catechism*, it involves "definitive self-exclusion from . . . God." Christianity has always maintained that the souls in hell are permanently locked in their eternal condition after they die. Once a person descends to hell, there is no transitioning from hell to purgatory, let alone to heaven. Hell is forever.

Fourth, God doesn't send people to hell, they choose it themselves. The *Catechism* used the term "self-exclusion" to affirm how people end up in hell. C. S. Lewis famously said that "the gates of hell are locked from the inside." In other words, hell is not a place into which an angry God thrusts people, locking the door and throwing away the key. We put ourselves into hell. We become so self-absorbed that we reject God, closing the door of our hearts and locking God out. Few people make a conscious choice for hell. But people decide on hell with their actions, the orientation of their lives, and addiction to unrepentant, serious sin.

Finally, hell is necessary if both God and free will exist. Some people imagine that the Church invented hell to scare people into submission, threatening them with eternal punishment. But the existence of hell is a logical corollary of two other truths: God's existence and our free will.

Here's the rationale: if God exists and we are free to say yes to him, then we must necessarily be free to say no to him and spend forever apart from him. So, hell is necessary if we have the freedom to say no to God and thus choose to be forever separated from him. That's what hell is—the rejection of God.

If you master those five facts, you'll have a clear understanding of hell and know how to respond when people misrepresent it.

To briefly recap:

- Hell exists.
- Hell is a state of being.
- Hell is definitive.
- Hell is a choice.
- Hell is necessary.

Expert Interview with Msgr. Charles Pope

➤ **Watch the interview here: https://claritasu.com/pope**

Msgr. Charles Pope serves as the pastor of Holy Comforter Saint Cyprian Catholic Church, which is a vibrant parish in the Archdiocese of Washington, D.C. He has led Bible studies in the US Congress and the White House. Msgr. Pope is a prolific Catholic blogger and writes a popular question-and-answer column in *Our Sunday Visitor Newsweekly*.

In this interview, Msgr. Pope responds to the following questions:

1. Why do you think Catholics and Church leaders rarely talk about heaven, hell, and purgatory?
2. What are some of the biggest misconceptions about heaven, and what should we know about it?
3. Why is it important that we talk about hell and affirm its existence and possibility?
4. How can we talk about hell without seeming abrasive?
5. When it comes discussing the Last Things with friends and family, what would you advise?

Excerpt from the Interview

"Heaven is not my personal designer paradise. It's the kingdom of God, and all of its fullness. It's what God loves and who God loves, and so, it involves values like chastity, mercy, forgiveness, love of neighbor, but also love of enemy. It involves some very challenging principles.

"The heart of heaven is to be with God. We were made to look on his glorious face. My heart speaks within me, 'seek, always, the face of the Lord,' and to just see God's beauty and be caught up in what the Eastern Church calls the *perichoresis*, the great dance of love and heaven, that's the heart of heaven." (Charles Pope)

WHAT WE KNOW ABOUT PURGATORY

Thus far, we have considered how to speak about heaven and hell with clarity and confidence. Let's turn next to purgatory. Like heaven and hell, purgatory is not a place but a state of being. Purgatory involves purgation, which means cleansing. If a person dies with the stain of sin on their soul, they must go through a purification process. You might think of it as a carwash for your soul that removes the last residue of sin and makes you fit to enter heaven. Purgatory is necessary because when most of us die, we are far from being perfect. We might generally love God and be virtuous to some degree, but we still have sinful inclinations that need to be purged. That's what purgatory does.

We should note that this simile limps mightily because it implies that purgatory is a place and that purgation is a temporal process that requires a specific amount of chronological time. But more on that in moment.

Let's look at a few important facts about purgatory. We know that many Catholics misunderstand purgatory, not to mention our non-Catholic relatives and friends. So, what facts should you emphasize in conversation?

Purgatory Is Not Punishment but Mercy

Don't think of purgatory as something to avoid; rather think of it as a good gift. Consider the following analogy. Suppose you were going to a fancy dinner party with your spouse or a friend, and you needed to shower to clean up after working in the yard all day. You would not complain about the shower as a punishment. Instead, you'd be thankful for the chance to cleanse yourself in order to appear at your best.

Similarly, purgatory is a chance—a merciful opportunity—to have our souls cleansed from sin so as to appear before God in heaven as pure, spotless sons and daughters. So, ultimately, purgatory is a gift for which we're grateful, not a punishment we want to avoid.

Purgatory Is Not an Eternal Destination

There are only two eternal states of being: heaven and hell. Heaven means you are in the presence of God, and hell means you are separate from God. Both of those states last forever. There is no eternal middle ground.

Purgatory is not some third alternative. It is a *temporary* cleansing of sin and twisted inclinations that people go through in order to prepare them for heaven. But no one stays in purgatory forever; they pass through purgatory on their way to heaven. People experiencing this purification after death have no possibility of going to hell. So, making it to purgatory is actually a reason for celebration, not disappointment.

That being said, the safety of purgatory sometimes makes people lower the bar of sanctity. With a dose of false humility, they pretend to be unworthy for heaven and just shoot for purgatory. But we should persuade such people that purgatory is not a goal but a process on the way to eternity. Tell them to aim higher!

Purgatory Is Definitely Biblical

You may have Protestant friends who claim that the Catholic Church invented the idea of purgatory and that it is not found anywhere in the Bible. But the truth is that purgatory does appear in both the Old Testament and the New Testament.

In the Old Testament, the clearest reference is in the book of 2 Maccabees. After a major battle in which many Jewish warriors died, a leader named Judas Maccabeus discerned that the soldiers died as a punishment for sin. So, he took up a collection and sent it to Jerusalem as a sin offering. "If he were not expecting the fallen to rise again, it would have been superfluous and foolish to pray for the dead. . . . Thus he made atonement for the dead that they might be absolved from their sin" (2 Mc 12:43–46). This passage shows that the Jews believed prayers and atonement by the living could deliver the dead from sin. What 2 Maccabees describes is close to the reality of purgatory.

Protestants, however, will not accept this reference because they do not consider 2 Maccabees as part of the

scriptures. It was one of the seven books the leaders of the
Protestant Reformation removed from the Bible. Even so,
the text provides historical evidence of something like purgatory in the Old Testament. Even if the Protestant rejects
this as divine scripture, they should at least acknowledge
it's a *historical* reference to early Jewish belief in a purga-
torial state.

The New Testament offers more explicit scriptural evidence for purgatory. For example, in the Sermon on the
Mount, Jesus says:

> Settle with your opponent quickly while on the
> way to court with him. Otherwise your opponent
> will hand you over to the judge, and the judge
> will hand you over to the guard, and you will
> be thrown into prison. Amen, I say to you, you
> will not be released until you have paid the last
> penny. (Mt 5:25)

Many of the earliest Christians saw this as a parable for
the experience of a soul in purgatory. For instance, the
Church Father Tertullian, writing around AD 200, notes
how "prison" is a common metaphor for purgatory.

More important, in this section of the Sermon on the
Mount, Jesus is focusing on the Last Things. He is teaching on heaven, hell, and mortal and venial sins. So, we can
interpret this parable as implying purgatory.

Finally, the plainest text in the scriptures comes from St.
Paul's first letter to the Corinthians:

> For no one can lay a foundation other than the
> one that is there, namely, Jesus Christ. If anyone
> builds on this foundation with gold, silver, pre-
> cious stones, wood, hay, or straw, the work of
> each will come to light, for the Day will disclose
> it. It will be revealed with fire, and the fire will
> test the quality of each one's work. If the work
> stands that someone built upon the foundation,
> that person will receive a wage. But if someone's
> work is burned up, that one will suffer loss; the
> person will be saved, but only as through fire. (1
> Cor 3:11–15)

This text clearly speaks about a judgment that will take place after death. But it can't be about heaven, because it implies that imperfections must be "burned up," and there can't be any imperfections in heaven. Also, the passage can't be about hell since it describes people being "saved," and people in hell are not and will never be saved.

Therefore, a third state of being must exist that purges people's imperfections before final salvation and their entry into the state of heaven. That state is purgatory.

So, let's recap the three facts about purgatory:

- Purgatory is not a punishment but mercy.
- Purgatory is not an eternal destination.
- Purgatory is biblical.

ANSWERING THE BEST OBJECTIONS

Next, let's look at the best objections you'll hear about the Last Things. We'll look at one each for heaven, hell, and purgatory.

Objection 1: "Heaven is just a wish-fulfillment fantasy. It's made up by people who can't handle the difficulties of life."

When you hear this objection, you should immediately point out that there is a difference between *whether* something exists and *why* someone believes in it. To make this case, simply turn the tables on the other person and say, "What if someone told you that atheism was a wish-fulfillment fantasy, that it's made up by people who want to avoid being judged for their behavior on earth?" Obviously, the person would not think this is a good argument against atheism (which is true), but this enables you to show how something might exist regardless of our desires or fantasies. The fact of heaven's existence has nothing to do with whether I want it to exist or not or whether it fulfills some desire.

You could explain that perhaps the critic has things backward. Perhaps heaven exists because God exists, and God planted in human beings a longing for heaven as their final home. In that case, what the critic calls a "wish-fulfillment fantasy" is actually more like homesickness. The fact that so many people yearn for heaven becomes evidence in its favor, not evidence against it.

Objection 2: "How could a loving God send people to hell?"

If God is all-loving and wants all people with him in heaven forever, why would he send anyone to hell? Why couldn't he just forgive everyone, no matter what they've done, and welcome them into heaven? These are perennial questions.

Based on what you learned earlier in this chapter, you should have a good idea about how to respond. First, you want to emphasize that God doesn't send people to hell; rather, they choose hell for themselves when they reject him.

Second, highlight the confusion that God's love and the existence of hell are somehow incompatible. This contention fails to understand that love requires free will. If God created people out of love, and people are truly free to say yes to that love, then they must logically be free to say no. Therefore, no incompatibility stands between God being all-loving and the existence of hell. In fact, one implies the other.

Objection 3: "Purgatory is not in the Bible."

We have seen that purgatory appears in both the Old and New Testaments, including the words of Jesus himself. Let me add another strong argument. When someone claims purgatory is not found in the scriptures, you should challenge the assumption that everything that Christians believe must be found explicitly in the Bible. If your opponent agrees that Christians can believe doctrines that are not explicitly stated in the scriptures, then you can immediately say that purgatory might be one of them.

But if a critic holds to the view that Christians should only believe things found explicitly in the Bible, you can turn their words against them. You can ask where the Bible explicitly teaches *that view*, that Christians must only accept what is explicitly taught in the Bible. This is an unanswerable objection because the Bible never teaches that.

You want to help the other person see that all Christians believe in truths not detailed in the Bible, such as the Trinity, the wrongness of abortion, and the immorality of nuclear war. We know those truths through other means, such as the authoritative teaching of the Church or through natural reasoning. The same holds with purgatory. This is a doctrine we can recognize not just through the scriptures but by the authority of the Church, which has taught it down through the centuries, or through natural reasoning.

TALKING TIPS AND STRATEGIES

Now that we know the basic facts about heaven, hell, and purgatory, and how to respond to the top objections, let's consider some practical tips and strategies to speak more effectively about these issues.

Tip 1: Don't overstate what we know about the Last Things.

In many ways, heaven, hell, and purgatory are incomprehensible. We know a lot about them, but we can't fully comprehend them—we can't wrap our minds fully around them.

Consider an analogy that illustrates this difficulty. In 1884, Edwin Abbott wrote a fascinating novella called *Flatland* about a two-dimensional world occupied by geometric figures. In his story, women are lines and men are polygons, but all are two-dimensional characters living in a flat, two-dimensional setting. At one point in the story, the main character, a Square, is visited by a three-dimensional Sphere. However, when the Square looks at the Sphere, he only sees a circle. That's the limit of his two-dimensional perspective.

The limited world of *Flatland* is something like our world in relation to heaven, hell, and purgatory. In a sense, those states of being are in a higher, different dimension. When we look at them or talk about them, we're only seeing a slice. Because we can't comprehend the full reality, our language and perspective will inevitably come up short.

So, when discussing the Last Things with friends and family, don't overstate what we know about them. We know some facts that we've received from God through the scriptures and the Church. But don't be afraid to admit that these realities are engulfed in mystery. Too much confidence may come across as arrogance and could backfire.

Tip 2: If people doubt purgatory, ask if they at least wish it were real.

This is a good test to see if they properly understand what purgatory is. If you ask whether they want purgatory to be real and they say no, chances are high they have some misconceptions about it. They would only answer no if they thought purgatory was a part of hell, that it wasn't beneficial, or that it didn't lead to heaven. But in this chapter, we have learned that purgatory is good, that it's not a punishment but mercy. Going to purgatory means you're on your way to heaven.

So, this is a good litmus test for whether the person really understands purgatory and if they don't, it gives you a chance to clarify any confusion.

Tip 3: Emphasize that God always gives people what they want in the end.

Many people see God as arbitrarily putting some people in heaven, others in purgatory, and the rest in hell. It's all kind of arbitrary on his part. But you must insist that *we*, not God, decide our eternal destinies.

Remember how the *Catechism* says that hell is "the state of definitive self-exclusion from communion with God and the blessed." Thanks to free will, it's possible that we can exclude ourselves from heaven, choosing to make our eternal home in hell. Conversely, we can say yes to God's invitation, put faith in Jesus as the Son of God, give ourselves entirely to him, take up our cross, and follow him, all of which results in our union with God in heaven. In either case, however, God gives us what we want: if we prefer hell, that's what we get; if we prefer him, he'll give us that instead.

RECOMMENDED BOOKS
(in order of importance)

Peter Kreeft, *Everything You Ever Wanted to Know About Heaven but Never Dreamed of Asking* (Ignatius Press, 1990).

> Dr. Kreeft devotes each chapter to clear and helpful answers to questions such as the following: What is heaven like? What will we do in heaven? Will we have bodies in heaven? Will there be animals in heaven? This is my favorite book on heaven written by one of my favorite authors.

Peter Kreeft, *Heaven, the Heart's Deepest Longing* (Ignatius Press, 1989).

> In this beautiful book, Dr. Kreeft meditates on our desire for heaven. He draws his reflections on this innate longing from philosophy, psychology, literature, music, and personal experience. My favorite chapter is near the end, in which he explains how belief in heaven affects our daily life.

Wade L. J. Menezes, C.P.M., *The Four Last Things: A Catechetical Guide to Death, Judgment, Heaven, and Hell* (EWTN Publishing, 2017).

> This is a clear, concise, straightforward look at what the Catholic Church teaches about death, judgment, heaven, and hell. Fr. Menezes unpacks what the *Catechism of the Catholic Church* teaches about each topic. Quotes from the scriptures and the saints pepper nearly every page.

C. S. Lewis, *The Great Divorce* (many editions).

This strange, funny, insightful, and profound novel tells of the main character's travels on a bus from the outskirts of hell—maybe purgatory—to the outskirts of heaven. With him are souls who are given a chance to decide whether they would like to stay or go back. Their conversations reveal the warped justifications people make for not wanting to enter heaven.

FOR REFLECTION AND DISCUSSION

1. Why do you think we find it difficult to talk about the Last Things? What are some ways to start speaking about them?
2. What is the best way to describe heaven?
3. What does the Catholic Church teach about heaven, hell, and purgatory?
4. How would you answer the objection that a good God would never send people to hell?
5. What is purgatory?
6. What would you say to someone who claims that purgatory is not in the Bible?

FOR PRACTICE

For each of the following scenarios, write a response using what you learned in this chapter.

1. Suppose a friend objects to the doctrine of hell: "You say God gives people what they want in the end, but is that really true? No one really wants hell, and if they knew that they were headed for hell, they would change. All of this is God's fault."

2. A friend or relative says, "Heaven is bound to get boring. Day after day of worship. Heck, one hour on Sunday is boring enough. Even if heaven is real, it just sounds like it would be misery after a while."

4

RELATIVISM

Relativism is one of the most prevalent and dangerous worldviews today, yet few Catholics are equipped to discuss it. Pope emeritus Benedict XVI spoke often about the "dictatorship of relativism," and Pope Francis has described relativism as "the spiritual poverty of our time."

It's almost certain that relativism has gained hold of many of your family members and friends. But how do you help them? This chapter will show you how to communicate the problems with relativism and how to escape it.

You will learn

- the definition of relativism and where it came from;
- how to respond to people who think truth and morality are relative;
- relativism's seven fatal flaws; and
- answers to the biggest objections you will hear from relativists.

By the time you reach the list of recommended books at the end of the chapter, you will feel equipped to deal with this deadly worldview.

WHAT IS RELATIVISM?

Suppose I asked you to name the most pressing challenge to faith today. Your answer might be atheism, radical Islam, the sexual revolution, or a number of other threats. But for many leaders of the Catholic Church, including the last few popes, the unequivocal answer is relativism.

Relativism is the view that there are no absolute facts about truth, goodness, or beauty. It holds that all claims are relative either to someone's personal beliefs or to their culture. For example, relativists will say, "If it's true for *you*, then great! But it's not necessarily true for *me*." Or "It might be right for *you*, but not for *me*." That's the personal form of relativism, where truth and morality are relative to individual people. There's also the cultural form, based on the same idea, which holds that, "If your culture says it's true, then it's true." Or "If your culture says it's good, then it's good."

Put another way, relativists believe there are no statements that are *absolutely* true for all people, at all times, and in all places. They think a particular truth, such as "God exists" or "there are only two genders," is only true some of the time, or for some people, or in some places. *You* might believe that God exists, which makes it true for you, but *other people* don't believe that God exists, therefore it's not true for them.

Similarly, as with truth, relativists believe all moral rules are flexible, such as "sex outside of marriage is wrong" or "we should not kill unborn children." They believe certain moral rules may apply to some people at some points in time, but in a different culture or at a different time those moral rules could flip.

You can see how relativism presents a serious problem, especially for Catholics. Because God is absolute and unchanging, Catholicism holds absolute truths and morals, such as "God exists," "Jesus is God," and "murder is wrong." But the whole foundation crumbles if those truths hold only for you or me or our culture, but not for other people in other places or times.

For the full-on relativist, all claims about truth and morality are nothing more than opinions. Religion is reduced to personal preference—you like Catholicism, I like atheism; you like chocolate, I like vanilla; you like rap music, I like classical. To be fair, relativists are right that *some* claims are relative, like which foods are best or which sports are most exciting. But not all beliefs are relative, and that's where relativism goes wrong.

To put it simply, relativism and Christianity are incompatible. That's what inspired Pope Benedict to denounce relativism with such forceful language. In April of 2005, during a homily at the Vatican moments before he was elected pope, he spoke of the world "moving towards a dictatorship of relativism which does not recognize anything as certain and which has as its highest goal one's own ego and one's own desires."[1]

The relativist doesn't look outside of himself to find truth, goodness, and beauty. Instead, he looks within himself, "to [his] own ego and [his] own desires." The standard of what's true, good, and beautiful is not God, the Bible, or the natural law—it's oneself. The relativist agrees with the ancient Greek philosopher Protagoras: Man is the measure.

A recent study from the Barna Research Group found that three out of four Americans (72 percent) are functional relativists, agreeing with this statement: "There is no such thing as absolute truth. Two people could define truth in totally conflicting ways, but both still be correct."[2] The same study found that roughly three-quarters of Americans (71 percent) agree: "There are no absolute standards that apply to everybody in all situations."[3]

Relativism is especially pervasive among younger generations. Philosopher and professor Allan Bloom said, "There is one thing a [college] professor can be absolutely sure of: almost every student entering the university believes, or says he believes, that truth is relative."[4]

So, why all this focus on relativism? Because relativists are the most difficult people you will ever engage about religion or morality. They will not forcefully disagree with you, challenge your views with surprising, unanswerable objections, nor will they attempt to poke holes in your arguments—just the opposite. They will rarely push back against your reasoning. Instead, they will grant your views with a dismissive smile, saying, "Well, if that's what you believe, then that's true for you. But that doesn't make it true for me."

Because of this, it's difficult to share fruitful dialogue with relativists. When you start discussing religion or morality, they won't be open to joining you in a shared pursuit of the truth, primarily because they don't believe there *is* an absolute truth to be discovered! Therefore, you need to be ready for these conversations. You must be able to spot relativism and respond to it with clarity and confidence.

IS THERE OBJECTIVE TRUTH?

Let's begin with a quick background on where relativism came from. You don't need to memorize these facts, but they'll be helpful as background knowledge.

Relativism has been a popular worldview for a long time. The Greek philosopher Protagoras taught a version nearly 500 years before Christ. He held that, "As each thing appears to me, so it is for me, and as it appears to you, so it is for you."[5] He also said, "Whatever view a city takes on [religious or moral] matters and establishes as its law of convention, is truth and fact for that city."[6]

Sources of Relativism

Although relativism has been present since Protagoras, it didn't gain major traction until the early twentieth century, with the scientific discoveries of Albert Einstein. In 1905, Einstein developed his two famous theories of general and special relativity. He found that within space and time, there is no single reference frame nor absolute standard in the universe. In other words, there's no absolute zero point in the universe. In the world of physics, everything is, indeed, relative.

However, many people, then and now, confused Einstein's scientific theory of relativity with the worldview of relativism. They assumed that if space and time are relative, then truth and morality must also be relative. Einstein repeatedly tried to correct this fallacy but without much success.

Objective and Subjective Truths

Thanks to this misinterpretation of Einstein, many people today believe there is no such thing as Truth with a capital "T." Instead, they think all truths are relative, "little-t" truths, ones that vary based on our personal beliefs, culture, experiences, or likes and dislikes.

It's important to distinguish between these two conceptions. "Big-T" Truth, or what we call objective truths, are absolute and hold for all people, in all places, and at all times. Some examples include slavery is wrong, the speed of light is 186,000 miles per second, and two plus two equals four. No sane person would claim that two plus two may be four *for you*, but for me two plus two is five. No, the sum of two and two is an objective truth, always the same for anyone, regardless of your background, opinions, or frame of reference.

Subjective truths, on the other hand—those "little-t" truths—are those that only hold in *some* cases. These are relative to some individual person, or group of people, or only at certain times. For example, the truth that chocolate ice cream is the best flavor, basketball is the most exciting sport, or children should always say "Yes, sir" or "Yes, ma'am" when speaking to an adult are examples of relative truths. Such truths might hold for one person in their particular context and time, but not for everyone, everywhere, at all times.

So, subjective ("little-t") truths are based on what's *inside* of you or your group, and therefore can change from person to person. Objective ("big-T") truths, on the other hand, exist *outside* of us. We don't invent objective truths—we discover them. They don't change or depend on our personal views.

Where Relativists Err

This brings us to the crux of the problem: relativists think *all* truth is subjective—they think all truths are "little-t" truths. But in almost every case, if you press them even a little, you will discover that they don't believe this deep down. When pressed, virtually all relativists will acknowledge in at least *some* objective ("big-T") Truths. For example, if you ask them whether mathematical and scientific truths are subjective or objective, they will usually admit they are objective, that they are absolute and unchanging. They will agree that the claim "two plus two equals four" is not dependent on personal opinion and that it's true for all people, in all places, at all times.

However, you will typically face resistance when it comes to religion and morality. Even if relativists admit that some truths in the realms of math and science are objective, they don't think religion and morality are in the same category. They believe that religion and morality are less like math and science and more like food or musical preferences.

Let's focus specifically on religion. Most relativists believe all religions teach truth, or that all religions are equally true, but sharp readers will observe these two claims are not the same, and you must distinguish between them. The belief that all religions teach truth is unobjectionable. No religion is entirely wrong about everything it teaches. All religions contain some degree of truth, otherwise no one would believe it.

But the claim that all religions are *equally* true is problematic, and it gets at the heart of why relativism fails. All religions can't be equally true because they make mutually exclusive claims. For example, Christianity teaches that Jesus of Nazareth is God, while Judaism and Islam deny that Jesus is God. So, considering just this one point, either Christianity is right and Judaism and Islam are wrong, or Christianity is wrong while Judaism and Islam are right. But all three religions cannot be equally true on this point.

Evil is another example. Christianity teaches that evil is real, while Buddhism teaches that evil is an illusion. Again, the two religions can't be equally true on this issue. One must be right, and one must be wrong. Such examples demonstrate that the realm of objective truth extends beyond math and science to religion as well.

IS MORALITY RELATIVE?

But what about morality? Even if you convince someone that religious claims are absolute, and not relative, what about moral claims?

Competing Moral Standards

Many think that right and wrong change depending on who you are or when and where you live. The most common cause of this view comes in the plain reality of moral disagreement among cultures. For instance, some seventeenth–century indigenous tribes in Canada considered it not just morally permissible but obligatory—even noble and honorable—to strangle elderly parents who became incapable of supporting themselves. If an elderly couple had no children to perform this ritual act, they would request that a friend's child kill them.[7] On the other hand, our culture today does not support the ritual murder of aged parents. However, some people believe these contradictory moral beliefs show that morality cannot not objective.

But just because two cultures disagree about a moral question that doesn't mean no objective answer exists. Consider an analogy from science. Even today, there is vast disagreement about all sorts of scientific questions from evolution to quantum mechanics. That doesn't mean answers don't exist for those questions. It just means that some (or maybe even all) scientists are currently confused or mistaken about the answer. In fact, science presupposes that objective answers exist, otherwise it would not pursue the questions in the first place.

Morality works in a similar way. Objective moral rules and duties exist, such as that murder is always wrong, and those tenets are true even if some people disagree with them or are mistaken about them. In those cases, we don't say such people merely share a different moral opinion. We say they are wrong.

So, it simply doesn't follow that a diversity of moral views means there's no objective moral standard. This is an important takeaway for you, and you'll want to keep it in mind when talking with relativists.

Undermining Moral Relativism

But we can press the case even further, showing that cultures actually agree about morality far more than they differ. In his book *The Abolition of Man*, C. S. Lewis includes an appendix that outlines what he calls the Tao. It describes the shared moral standard that virtually all cultures and major religions have adopted throughout history. For instance, Lewis notes that there is no record of a culture that praises cowardice and treason as good. He lists many more examples of moral behaviors that cultures universally agree are vices and not virtues.

But suppose, for a moment, that someone nevertheless embraces moral relativism. Then what? Well, a next step is to focus on the disastrous effects of that worldview. What happens when people believe that no culture, state, or religion can determine morality but that it's up to each individual to decide what's right and wrong?

The answer is violence. Look to the twentieth century for several examples of relativism in action, from Marxism to Nazism, and the millions of resulting corpses. Any system of morality rooted in mere personal opinions inevitably results in hostility. Because no outside, absolute standard of morality exists, aggression becomes the only way to settle moral disputes, with the stronger party prevailing—"might makes right."

Thankfully, upon a little reflection, most people reject this outcome. They realize stronger people should not set the moral rules simply because they're bigger or better armed than weaker people. But if they reject the outcome, they have to reject the principle that inevitably produces it—they have to reject relativism.

Expert Interview with Francis J. Beckwith

➤ **Watch the interview here: https://claritasu.com/beckwith**

Dr. Beckwith is Professor of Philosophy at Baylor University. His faith journey has been from the Catholicism of his youth to Evangelicalism as an adult and then back to the Catholic Church. He is the author of numerous books, including *Return to Rome: Confessions of an Evangelical Catholic* and *Never Doubt Thomas: The Catholic Aquinas as Evangelical and Protestant*. He's also the coauthor, with Gregory Koukl, of *Relativism: Feet Firmly Planted in Mid-Air*.

In this interview, Dr. Beckwith responds to the following questions:

1. How would you define relativism? What does a relativist believe?
2. As a college professor, do you find that most young people today are functionally relativists?

3. Where has relativism come from? Why has it become so prevalent?
4. What would be your first move to respond to a family member or friend who has embraced relativism?
5. What would you say to someone who calls you intolerant because you hold absolute views?
6. Given the absurd ramifications of relativism, what would the world be like if all people adopted relativism?
7. What tips would you give Catholics when they're talking with friends or family about relativism?

Excerpt from the Interview

"Another tactic for responding to a relativist would be to simply come up with a counter example. Suppose you're sitting in a room with two people, Mother Teresa and Adolf Hitler, and you discover that they actually have deep disagreement about human dignity. Would it be appropriate for Mother Teresa to say, 'Well that's just true for you, Adolf, but not true for me.' Or would it be better for her to say, 'No, in fact, engaging in genocide is simply deeply wicked, for everybody'?" (Francis J. Beckwith)

RELATIVISM'S SEVEN FATAL FLAWS

In Francis Beckwith's book *Relativism: Feet Firmly Planted in Mid-Air,* which he coauthored with Protestant apologist Gregory Koukl, he presents seven fatal flaws of relativism.[8]

If you master and memorize even just one of these, you will be able to demonstrate why relativism is untenable.

Fatal Flaw 1: Relativists Can't Accuse Others of Wrongdoing

If relativism is true, nothing is right or wrong for everyone. Therefore, you surrender the possibility of making moral judgments about other people or cultures. As a relativist, you can't say that what someone did is truly wrong. At best, you can only say that you don't like their actions or that their behavior offends your personal sense of right and wrong. So, relativists can't accuse someone of wrong behavior.

Fatal Flaw 2: Relativists Can't Complain about the Problem of Evil

It's hard to determine why there is so much evil in the world—murder, rape, and preventable human suffering. But if relativism is true, then none of these things are truly wrong—just personally distasteful—and the problem of evil fizzles away. In other words, you can't be a relativist and simultaneously complain about evil and suffering. You have to either give up your relativism and admit some things are objectively wrong, or you must stop grumbling about the problem of evil.

Fatal Flaw 3: Relativists Can't Accept Praise or Place Blame

We praise someone's moral behavior when it meets some standard of excellence. For example, we *praise* a man who jumps in front of a gunman to prevent a mass shooting, because we recognize that sacrificing your life to save others is objectively good. On the flip side, we would *blame* someone who sees a woman being raped on the sidewalk and chooses not to intervene or call the police, because we know that such behavior is objectively wrong. However, relativism has no objective moral standard against which to assign praise or blame. So, for relativists, moral behaviors are not good, better, bad, or worse—they just *are*. They can't place blame or assign praise.

Fatal Flaw 4: Relativists Can't Make Charges of Unfairness or Injustice

The concept of justice always requires an absolute standard that determines the way things ought to be. For example, it's unjust that young children are kidnapped and sold into the sex trade because children ought not to be enslaved and abused. But if relativism were true, there would be no objective moral facts and therefore no absolute standard that defines the way things ought to be. So, relativists are not able to say something is unfair or unjust. At most, they can say, "I don't like that."

Fatal Flaw 5: Relativists Can't Improve Their Morality

Most of us strive to be good people and, even more, to become better people as we age. We want to display moral improvement, but we need a standard by which to measure it. For example, to raise your grades in math class, you must have a scale to gauge improvement, so you can tell that you jumped from an 82 percent B to a 94 percent A.

The same works in the moral life. You can improve morally only when you have an absolute standard, an objective way to identify moral perfection and your progress either toward that goal or away from it. But again, relativists have no absolute moral standard and therefore no way to improve their morality. Their moral behavior doesn't get better or worse over the years, it just changes, differing from year to year. Their moral behavior might vary, but it can't improve.

Fatal Flaw 6: Relativists Can't Hold Meaningful Moral Discussions

When we discuss morality, we often compare the merits of two different moral ideas to determine which is best. For example, in a severe famine, where there is not enough food to go around, people might ask whether it would be better to feed the sick and elderly or to just let them die, so they don't drain the community's resources. To answer that question, we would need to measure each view against a shared moral framework, one that must include objective facts, such as the value and dignity of human life.

But if relativism is true and all moral views are equal, then what's there to talk about? The relativist has no standard by which to compare two different moral positions and determine which one is better. Having a moral discussion or debate is pointless.

Fatal Flaw 7: Relativists Can't Promote the Obligation of Tolerance

Our culture celebrates tolerance as a premiere virtue. This is especially the case for relativists. They believe that with so many different moral views around the world, we ought to tolerate every moral opinion and behavior.

But this attempt to promote tolerance is self-contradictory. The moment the relativist contends that we *ought* to tolerate the moral opinions of other people, they're appealing inadvertently to an absolute moral truth. They're making a moral rule that everyone *ought* to follow.

However, relativism allows no such universal rules. Therefore, relativists can't promote the obligation of tolerance and remain relativists. They can't say everyone *must* be tolerant. At most they can say it's their personal opinion that people should be tolerant, but they can't make it an obligatory rule for everyone.

I hope that these seven fatal flaws have given you several angles of attack, multiple ways to undercut relativism. Pick your favorite flaw—maybe the one you find easiest to remember—and use it in conversations to help relativists see the truth.

ANSWERING THE BEST OBJECTIONS

Next, let's look at some of the best objections you will face from relativistic friends and family. Consider them now, and you won't be surprised when you meet them in conversation.

Objection 1: "Most people disagree about morality, so there can't be one right moral code for everyone."

Relativists typically advance this objection. They contend that every country has different moral opinions, and that cultures throughout history have had vastly different moral codes. With so much disagreement about right and wrong, they speculate that morality can't be objective.

To respond, apply that same logic to other areas of disagreement. For example, you might ask if there is one correct view of evolution or if evolution is objectively true. In my experience, most people will say yes. But in that case, you can point out that many people disagree about evolution. In fact, about 50 percent of Americans say they believe in evolution and 50 percent reject it. Does the fact that so many people disagree about evolution means that it's untrue? Pause for a moment and wait for them to connect the dots.

This approach exposes the relativist's logic as a non sequitur, meaning that their premises fail to support their conclusion. The main premise is that many people have differing moral views, but it doesn't follow that there must not be an objective moral code. That's an unfounded leap of logic.

I used evolution in the example, but you could use any controversial belief that the other person accepts. For example, they may ardently believe that human beings should not pollute the planet, or perhaps that abortion is permissible. Regardless of whether these claims are true, the key is to show the other person that many people disagree about these topics. Yet disagreement doesn't mean there is no right answer. It just means that some of the people are wrong about their views.

Objection 2: "Who are you to judge? It's arrogant to think you have the truth and everyone else is wrong. I don't think it's right to judge other people's moral opinions."

By and large, our culture believes that if you hold a definitive view about truth or morality, you think that you are 100 percent right and everyone else is 100 percent wrong. Implying others are wrong may be offensive.

When someone accuses you of this, of judging others so harshly, you can respond in several ways. First, when discussing whether something is true or good, we aren't judging *people*. We're only judging the truth of certain *beliefs* or the morality of certain *behaviors*. You should emphasize that we must separate people from their beliefs and behaviors. We can judge particular beliefs or behaviors—we all do this, including relativists—but we should never judge a person's soul, since only God can do that.

Second, it's not arrogant to think you're right about something. Everyone thinks their beliefs are right. Otherwise, why would they continue holding them? No one holds to beliefs they know are wrong. You can show this is the case by asking your objector this question: "You think all truths are relative, right? But I think some truths are *not* relative. So, do you think I'm wrong?" If the person says, "Yes, you're wrong," then you can reply, "Well, is that not arrogant on your part, at least according to your standard, to think that I'm wrong and you're right?" So, you can use their own criticism against them.

Finally, make it clear that disagreement isn't a zero-sum game, as if my being right means everyone else is one hundred percent wrong. That would indeed be extremely arrogant, if that's what we believed, but thankfully it's not. Everyone holds a mixture of true and false beliefs, including me and you. Just because I think people are wrong about one particular belief, it doesn't mean they're wrong about everything else. They may be mistaken only on this one point. So, once again, it's not arrogant to have confidence in your own beliefs, or to think other people might be wrong.

Objection 3: "We should all just be tolerant. Why can't you be tolerant of other people's beliefs, morals, or religion?"

As we've already noted, our culture places a high value on tolerance, but here's a key point: we only tolerate views that we disagree with. Tolerance, by its nature, *assumes* disagreement. It supposes that two views, two people, or two lifestyles are fundamentally incompatible.

This is a problem for relativists. They can't be tolerant of anyone because, for them, there's actually nothing to disagree with! For relativists, no conflict exists between two opposing views because they think both views are equally right, so there's nothing to tolerate. Therefore, it becomes

clear that a person can't support both relativism *and* tolerance. They have to choose one or the other.

Here's another tactic: if a relativist says, "We should
all be tolerant," then you can reply, "Well, are you saying
that's a moral duty, that all people should be tolerant?" If
the answer is, "Yes," then you can say, "Great! That's an
objective moral claim. You and I at least can agree on that,
that there are some objective moral facts, that not all morality is relative."

Objection 4: "I'm personally against that behavior, but I would never tell other people how to behave."

You hear this often, especially with hot-button moral issues,
such as abortion: "I'm personally against abortion, but I
would never stop other people from having abortions by
making it illegal." This sort of thinking only makes sense
if we presume that all moral questions are matters of subjective preference, like your favorite drink. I might prefer
soda, but I'm not going to force everyone to drink soda or
make it illegal to drink non-sodas.

Your goal here is to show the other person that morality
is less like subjective drink preferences and more like objective mathematical rules. To do this, you might say something like, "Tell me what you think about this. Suppose I
said, 'I personally think slavery is wrong, but I'm not going
to tell you to stop owning slaves or make slavery illegal.'
What would you think about that line of reasoning?"

Your partner will likely balk and say that slavery is always wrong. Then you can say, "Ah, then you and I agree. Our rejection of slavery isn't just a private, personal opinion. We agree that slavery is objectively wrong. But if that's the case, then morality isn't completely relative, right?"

Reflect on the responses to these objections and you will be able to deal with them clearly and confidently.

TALKING TIPS AND STRATEGIES

Let's consider four tips that will help you stay in control of any conversation with a relativist.

Tip 1: Ask the other person how to determine what is true or good.

This diagnostic question will help you determine whether the other person is truly a relativist. You want to ascertain whether the person relies on an objective standard, such as God or the natural moral law, or establish whether the person trusts a subjective standard, such as their own feelings, experience, intuitions, gut sense, opinion, or the laws of their particular country.

Especially listen for feeling-based language. If your opponent just "feels that something is right or wrong," chances are high that they embrace some sort of relativism, one based on their own subjective moods. In any case, once you detect relativism, then turn to the second tip below.

Tip 2: Ask what the person thinks about people whose feelings or experiences lead them to opposite conclusions from their own.

For example, suppose your dialogue partner feels that abortion is okay, but you, on the other hand, believe that abortion is evil. Both can't be right. So, you should ask, "How do we settle this dispute?" This question will force the other person to confront the obvious problem with relativism. With no outside standard to appeal to, the relativist cannot determine who is right.

Tip 3: Expose the self-contradictions in relativism.

You can set this up by asking something like, "So, I want to make sure I understand your view. Do you think there is no such thing as absolute truth? That everything is relative?" If the person says yes, then you can respond, "Well, do you think *that belief* is absolutely true, or is it only true for you?" If the answer is that it's true for everyone, then the person doesn't really embrace relativism. But if the response is that it's only true for the person, then you can say, "Great! Then moral relativism is not absolutely true, so I don't have any reason to believe in it myself."

Be delicate about this, because the goal isn't to create a "gotcha" moment in which you leave the other person feeling defeated and embarrassed. You want to help them to see the inherent contradictions in relativism.

Tip 4: Help your conversation partner find at least one objective truth.

With this strategy, we are moving past showing relativism's problems and helping the other person embrace objective truth and morality. To do this, you want to help them find at least one objective truth.

The one I have found most effective is the assertion that "torturing toddlers for fun is wrong." I introduced this universally accepted truth in the earlier chapter on faith and science. I've yet to meet a person who disagrees with this or who denies that this is a moral fact that holds for all people, at all times, in all places. It's simply wrong for anyone, anywhere to torture young children for fun. But if that's the case, then moral relativism can't be totally true. There must be some absolute moral facts.

If this example doesn't work, try this one: "Is it objectively true that Mother Teresa was a better person than Adolf Hitler?" Or "Is it objectively true that men should not rape women?"

Another approach is to home in on the other person's own hot-button moral concern, whether it's racism, animal rights, gun control, intolerance, LGBT concerns, or feminism, and then relativize it. You might say, "I know you're against racism, but as I'm sure you know, other people disagree. Isn't it intolerant and judgmental to say racists are wrong? Maybe they just have different feelings about the issue than you, right? So, how can you say they're wrong?" (You of course want to ask these questions with tongue in cheek, so as not to deceive the person into thinking you actually agree with these absurd positions. You're only using them hypothetically to expose the flaws of relativism.)

Your goal is to show that everyone holds to at least some absolute views, whether about truth or morality. Once the other person realizes that, their relativism will begin to crumble.

RECOMMENDED BOOKS
(in order of importance)

Edward Sri, *Who Am I To Judge?: Responding to Relativism with Logic and Love* (Ignatius Press, 2017).

> Dr. Sri describes many forms of relativism, gives a framework showing that Catholic morality is about love and is not judgmental, and presents seven keys for responding to relativism. He illustrates his message with anecdotes and real-world stories. I think this is the best Catholic book on dealing with relativism.

Francis J. Beckwith and Gregory Koukl, *Relativism: Feet Firmly Planted in Mid-Air* (Baker Books, 1998).

> Dr. Beckwith and Protestant apologist Koukl outline the fatal flaws of relativism and how to expertly handle conversations with relativists. The book devotes two lengthy sections to relativism's effect on education and on public policy, specifically in regard to marriage and abortion. It makes a strong case that when relativism holds sway in the culture, barbarism or tyranny naturally follow.

Peter Kreeft, *A Refutation of Moral Relativism: Interviews with an Absolutist* (Ignatius Press, 1999).

Dr. Kreeft creates a wide-ranging and funny fictional dialogue between Isa, a Muslim fundamentalist who defends moral absolutism, and Libby, a sassy feminist whose arguments for moral relativism don't hold up. An entertaining, enlightening, and accessible book.

Chris Stefanick, *Absolute Relativism: The New Dictatorship and What to Do About It* (Catholic Answers, 2011).

Chris's question-and-answer format allows you to quickly scan through the book to find whatever topics most interest you. It responds to the most common relativistic slogans. And the book also includes great practical tips, such as being careful not to qualify statements about truth and morality by saying, "Well, it's my opinion that . . ." and instead just stating the truth or moral claim as a fact, without qualification.

FOR REFLECTION AND DISCUSSION

1. What is relativism and why is it dangerous?
2. Why is the relativist the most difficult person to engage?
3. What is the difference between subjective and objective truth?
4. Why is it a problem to say that all religions are equally true?

5. What is personal moral relativism and how would you challenge it?
6. Why can't a relativist promote tolerance?

FOR PRACTICE

For each of the following scenarios, write a response using what you learned in this chapter.

1. Suppose a friend objects by saying, "Christians are way too judgmental. Why not just let people live the way they want and be happy? From what I've seen, Christians introduce burdens and artificial rules that just spoil the fun of life."

2. Suppose a family member says, "There's just no correct answer to some moral issues. When it comes to abortion for example, some top experts think it's totally ethical while some don't. People of different cultures and different educational backgrounds will inevitably disagree. There's no objective truth about the situation, and even if there was, there's no way we're going to be able to know it."

5

ISLAM

If you are like most Catholics, two things trouble you about Islam. First, you don't know much about it. You might be aware of the Quran or Muhammed, and you might be convinced that Islam encourages violence. Beyond that, you don't know enough to discuss it intelligently. Second, talking about Islam with friends and family is like walking through a minefield. You're worried about saying the wrong thing because the prevailing view of our culture is that it's politically incorrect to criticize Islam in any way.

So, if you're like most Catholics, for those two reasons you're reluctant to talk about it. But this chapter will relieve you of these concerns. It will give you the essential information you need in order to discuss Islam intelligently, accurately, and sensitively.

You will learn

- the key facts about Islam;
- how to discuss the main differences between Christianity and Islam;
- how to evangelize a Muslim friend or family member; and
- how to answer the big Muslim objections to Christianity.

ISLAM 101

Let's begin by looking at Muhammed and the Quran, the two most important parts of Islam.

Muhammed

Muhammed, the great prophet of Islam, was born around AD 570. An Arab, he was orphaned as a child and raised by an uncle, who was a caravan trader in Mecca in present-day Saudi Arabia. Like his uncle he became a merchant. At the age of twenty-five Muhammed married a wealthy widow, who was around forty years old at the time, and she bore him six children.

In his late thirties, he retired from trading and became interested in religion. Mecca had become a major outpost along the Silk Road, and there Muhammed encountered people from many religions, including heretical Christians. This gave Muhammed a sampling of different religious beliefs that helps explain the mishmash of traditions found in Islam.

The pivotal event in Muhammed's life occurred in AD 610, when he was around forty years old. While he was meditating in a cave on the outskirts of Mecca, suddenly a strange, spiritual being appeared, grabbed and shook him, and demanded he read a sentence written in the sand. Terrified, Muhammed explained that he couldn't read. But the being miraculously enabled him to read the words that gave a short prophecy about his future life.

Muhammed ran home and told his wife and relatives about the encounter. His wife's cousin interpreted the experience, telling him that the being was the archangel Gabriel. Afterward, he had more encounters with the angel, who revealed that he, Muhammed, was the "seal of the prophets," the final prophet of God. The angel assured Muhammed that his revelations would be perfect, complete, and final. These angelic revelations were eventually collected and became the Quran, Islam's holy book.

Muhammed claimed to receive these revelations for twenty-two years, from AD 610 until his death in AD 632. After his death, stories about his life began to circulate in various books, and these biographies also became sacred texts to Muslims. To this day, Muslims regard Mohammed as the perfect man, the ideal of Islamic belief and life. When a debate arises over a question or behavior, the answer can be found by asking, what would Muhammed do?

However, many critics have observed that Muhammed's life was far from perfect, at least by our moral standards today. Muhammed was guilty of robbery, extortion, sexual assault, pedophilia, contract killings, and mass murder.[1] But Muslims usually try to justify or downplay these many problems.

During the first half of his revelatory period, from AD 610 to 622, Muhammed proclaimed these angelic messages in Mecca and began growing the religion of Islam. But in AD 622, he angered many local Arabs who drove him into exile. He landed in Medina, where he demanded that the local Jewish population convert to Islam. When they refused, he changed his peaceful message into one of violence and began to preach forcefully against the Jews and all his opponents.

Muhammed eventually built a large army that helped him conquer the entire western Arabian coastline. After his death, that army grew and attempted to master the entire known world. From roughly AD 632 to 732, Muslim armies conquered most of the Middle East and much of Europe. Were it not for a heroic French resistance in AD 732, Europe would possibly be Muslim today.

The Quran

Next to Muhammed, the other most important feature of Islam is the Quran, their holy book. But for Muslims, the Quran is not merely a book of teachings. It contains the literal, uncreated, eternal Word of Allah (God). Muslims believe the Quran has always existed within Allah's mouth and was perfectly communicated to Muhammed.

The book includes 114 chapters, called *suras*. And these messages were given to Muhammed in an Arabic dialect that was unique to his region. This is very important, because Muslims do not believe that translations of the Quran are, properly speaking, the Word of Allah. The Quran is Allah's word only in the original Arabic. They believe that when this version is recited aloud, it has a mysterious, enchanting effect on listeners. This is why Muslims proclaim the Quran through loud bullhorns and speakers, especially to non-Muslims. They are convinced that merely listening to the Quran in Arabic will stir people's hearts and attract them to Islam, even if the listeners don't understand any of the words.

The teachings of the Quran are similar in style to the Old Testament, with stories, laws, and prophecies. However, the Quran doesn't follow a linear narrative structure with a beginning, middle, and end. It's more disjointed. The Quran's central theme is the ultimacy of God—that Allah alone deserves submission. In Arabic, the word *Islam* literally means "submission," and that sums up the central message of Islam: submission to God.

Even just a few minutes reading the Quran will expose many inconsistencies and contradictions, but Muslims rarely question them for two reasons. First, because Muslims believe the Quran is the literal Word of God, to question it is an act of blasphemy, which no serious Muslim would ever do. Second, rules of logic and reason do not bind Allah, as we'll explore more in a moment. God is beyond logic, so Muslims see no problem with him contradicting something he said or did earlier in the Quran.

A final important feature is that the Quran is based on and adapted from the Bible, in addition to ancient Jewish and heretical Christian texts. It references several figures and events from the scriptures, and it includes many Old Testament prophets. You will even find Jesus and his mother, Mary, both of whom the Quran deeply reverences. In fact, Islam regards Jesus as a major prophet.

Beliefs and Practices

All devout Muslims follow the five core beliefs and the five practices, or pillars, of Islam. Understanding these ten elements is key to understanding how Muslims live out their faith.

The Five Core Beliefs

First, Allah. Islam proclaims one God, Allah. For Muslims, the primary sin is worshipping other gods or committing blasphemy.

Second, the prophets. Muslims believe that God has revealed himself to thousands of prophets throughout history, but they identify twenty-five primary prophets. Adam is number one, then Enoch, then Noah, and so on, until you get to Jesus, who is number twenty-four, and then finally Muhammed, who is number twenty-five, the last prophet, the "seal of the prophets." Muslims hold that these prophets had one fundamental and consistent message: repent and return to Allah.

Third, angels and demons. Islam teaches the existence of an active spiritual world. Many Muslims hold that each of us is given a good angel, who records our good deeds, and a bad angel, who records our mistakes. During prayer, Muslims will sometimes turn and address these two angels.

Fourth, the holy books. These include the Quran, the most sacred book, but also the Torah from the Jews (the Old Testament), and even the *Injil,* which is the Islamic word for the gospels of the New Testament. However, Muslims are convinced that Jews and Christians have corrupted their biblical texts, and the Quran was needed to restore their true message. This is why quoting Christian scriptures to a Muslim is often met with skepticism.

Fifth, the final judgment. Muslims, like Christians, believe different things about heaven and hell, but all Muslims agree there will be a judgment at the end of time. Based on the way we live, we will either be rewarded or condemned.

The Five Pillars

Next to these five core beliefs, there are also the five pillars of Islam. First, the confession, also known as the *shahada*. This foundational statement of faith says, "There is no God but Allah, and Muhammed is the Apostle of Allah." This is the fundamental message of Islam. Muslims repeat it multiple times, every day. In fact, to become a Muslim, all you have to do is repeat the *shahada* three times.

Second, the prayers. Muslims perform Islam's ritual prayer five times a day, similar to the Liturgy of the Hours for Catholics. When they pray, Muslims always face Mecca, the city of Muhammed (similar to how Christian churches traditionally faced east for prayer). Islamic prayers include a recitation of verses from the Quran along with the *shahada* confession. The prayers earn merit and remove sin.

Third, fasting during Ramadan. For one month each year, Muslims fast from all food, water, and sexual relations from sunrise to sundown. This practice distinguishes them from the followers of other religions and demonstrates their moral and ascetic superiority. Even unfaithful, nonpracticing Muslims often observe the fast.

Fourth, giving alms. Muslims are expected to give 2.5 percent of their overall income to the poor each year. This almsgiving is critical because the Quran specifically ties it to salvation for Muslims.

Fifth, the pilgrimage to Mecca. Each Muslim must, if able, make a pilgrimage to Mecca at least once in his life. While there, a Muslim is expected to say special prayers and circle and touch, if possible, the great black rock, known as the Kaaba, which they believe was sent from heaven to Islam as a sacred place.

These five core beliefs and five core practices are the ways Muslims earn the favor of God. As Muslims often experience, however, they can become burdensome. Unlike Christianity, which is a religion of grace working through love, Islam is a religion based almost purely on works. A Muslim has to strive to earn God's favor and always lives in fear of not having done enough to satisfy Allah's demands.

CHRISTIANITY VERSUS ISLAM

So, now we understand the basics about Islam. You don't need to memorize all those features. It's mainly just helpful background information for the advice and strategies to come. But after getting up to speed on Islam, you next want to understand the major differences between Christianity and Islam, which will definitely help your conversations.

First, Both Religions Understand God Differently

Later in this chapter, we will address whether Muslims and Christians worship the same God in detail. In one sense, the answer is yes. They both follow the God of Abraham, Isaac, and Jacob, as revealed to the Israelites.

While Muslims and Christians both worship the same God, however, they have very different conceptions of him. These conceptions are contradictory, which means they can't both be true. For example, Christians believe God is a Trinity, one God in three divine persons—Father, Son, and Holy Spirit. Muslims reject this view, which they regard as blasphemy. They are convinced there is God in just *one* person. They do not think that Jesus is God—he is just a human prophet—and they don't believe in the Holy Spirit.

Second, Christians and Muslims Relate to God Differently

Christianity teaches that God is love, that he is a God of forgiveness and mercy who desires only that we know and love him in this life and enjoy him in the next. For Muslims, however, God is defined not by love but by his power, supremacy, and transcendence. Therefore, Muslims do not respond to him with love but with absolute submission. They relate to God less like children do to a divine father, as Christians do, and more like slaves or servants to a powerful ruler.

Third, the Religions Disagree on the Relationship between God and Truth

Christians believe something is true if it corresponds to the mind of God, because God is truth itself. Likewise, actions are good when they conform to God's nature, since God is also pure goodness.

On the other hand, Muslims think something is true simply because God commands it to be true, not because it corresponds to God's nature. They believe something is good because God says it is good. In either case, though, God could, at a later time, change his mind and declare the opposite to be true or good.

Let's consider an example. Early in the Quran, God commands Muslims to treat non-Muslims with respect and live peaceably with them. Later in the Quran, however, God encourages violence toward non-Muslims. Christians would say this is contradictory and makes God seem capricious or changeable. But Muslims admit no contradiction since goodness and truth are based on whatever God says, and if God wants to change his mind, he can. If he says rape is evil today, then it's evil today. But if tomorrow he says rape is good, then it becomes good.

This makes discussions between Christians and Muslims extremely difficult. Christians believe in a God of reason and consistency. Muslims believe God is not bound to reason for that would put a limitation on God. They do not expect God to act consistently according to our rational understanding, since his ways are inscrutable.

Fourth, the Two Religions Have Opposite Views about Jesus

Christians believe that Jesus is divine, the Son of God, whereas Muslims, although they reverence Jesus, consider him only as one human prophet among many.

Surprisingly, they also deny that Jesus was ever crucified and killed. The Quran says that Jesus' enemies "slew him not nor crucified him, but it appeared so unto them." In other words, the man that was crucified on the Cross was not Jesus but an imposter. Some Muslim scholars speculate it was a twin brother of Jesus, others say it was a lookalike, and still others suggest it may have been a stand-in who was magically made to look like Jesus. In any case, Muslims not only deny that Jesus is God, they also deny Jesus was killed on the Cross.

Fifth, Christianity and Islam View Their Sacred Texts Differently

Both religions are based on divinely inspired books, the Bible and the Quran. We Christians believe the Bible was inspired by God, which means it contains the Word of God expressed in the words of men. God inspired the authors to write each book, but human authors composed the actual words.

Muslims believe something very different about the Quran. They're convinced the Quran was divinely dictated. In other words, they think it contains the exact words that Allah spoke through an angel to Muhammed. Muhammed didn't interpret these words or express them in a particular culture or context. He merely copied the words down—he transcribed.

These differences have enormous implications for how we understand these sacred texts. For instance, consider how Christians and Muslims each view the Bible. Christians trust the Bible as reliable and accurate. But Muslims believe that both the Old and New Testaments in their original languages were originally pure and trustworthy, but that Jews and Christians corrupted the texts through translation and interpretation. So, the Bibles that we read today are fallible and contain errors, sometimes intentional.

The Quran encourages Muslims to respect the Bible, but if at any point the Bible contradicts the teachings of Islam, which it does several times, then Muslims are to believe that Christians or Jews introduced errors on purpose.

Now that we have considered the main differences between Christianity and Islam, let's recap them:

- Christians believe in the Trinity. Muslims are unitarians, which means they deny the Trinity.

- Christians see God's essence as love, while the Islamic God is defined by his power, supremacy, and transcendence.

- Christians believe God's truth and goodness are unchangeable while Muslims believe God can arbitrarily redefine truth and goodness.

- Christians believe that Jesus is divine, that he died on the Cross, and was raised from death; Muslims don't think

Jesus is God, nor do they think he was crucified, much less raised from the dead.

- Christians believe the scriptures were inspired by God but written in the words of men. Muslims think the Quran was dictated by God directly to Muhammed and that the Bible has been corrupted over time by Jews and Christians.

Keep these differences in mind not only when discussing Islam with fellow Christians but especially when talking with a Muslim friend or family member. These points of disagreement will shape how you discuss Christianity and how you should propose the Gospel to them. In fact, that's where we'll turn next: how to have fruitful, evangelistic conversations with a Muslim.

HOW TO EVANGELIZE A MUSLIM

Now that we have reviewed basic information about Islam and have considered the differences between Christianity and Islam, let's consider what's involved in evangelizing a Muslim. You may not have any Muslim friends at the moment, but based on the demographic data, you likely will soon. Muslims are among the fastest growing groups in the Western world, thanks mostly to immigration and high birth rates. So, you will want to be prepared to speak with them about the Gospel.

What Not to Do

Let's begin with how *not* to have these conversations. When talking with a Muslim, it's usually not effective to point out inconsistencies within Islam. When I first began studying Islam myself, this was the angle I thought was most promising. If you could show a Muslim how the Quran is wrong about key historical facts, such as the Crucifixion of Jesus, then that would cause them to doubt the whole Quran, and maybe doubt their whole faith. Or if you could show how parts of the Quran contradict other parts, then surely a Muslim would second-guess his sacred text.

But experience has taught me that inconsistencies don't present a major problem for most Muslims because they don't think God or religion must correspond to reason. As we have seen, they believe Allah can contradict himself or change his mind about statements of truth, and it won't help to show inconsistencies between the Quran and the Bible. If the Bible and the Quran contradict each other, Muslims think Christians intentionally twisted the scriptures to make Islam look bad.

Three Strategies for Evangelizing Muslims

So, what should we do instead? Missionaries to the Muslim world affirm that the most effective strategies focus on three approaches: cleansing the heart, opening up the Bible, and overcoming works righteousness.

The Cleanliness Strategy

Muslims have an intricate system of ritual cleanliness that is in some ways even more intense than that of the Jews of the Old Testament. For example, in order to participate in the obligatory Islamic prayers, Muslims have to undergo a complicated procedure of washing from head to neck to arms to feet, using a special mixture of water and sand. If at any point Muslims accidentally touch an unclean item, such as blood, excrement, or alcohol, they have to start the washing all over again. Muslims spend much of their day cleansing themselves and preventing impurity.

Former Muslims admit this relentless cleansing is a heavy burden. And this is why Christianity can be very liberating to Muslims. It teaches that the way to purity is not cleansing your body but your heart. As Jesus says, "There is nothing outside a man which by going into him can defile him; but the things which come out of a man are what defile him" (Mk 7:15; RSVCE).

Islam teaches the opposite. While it features rules and systems for cleansing the body, it offers very little to clean the darkness of our hearts. This failure is an unspoken concern among Muslims. They have no way to rid themselves of sinful thoughts or hidden flaws. They can try to repent, but the impurities remain because their own actions aren't enough to remove them.

Many Muslims realize they need something more, something absolutely pure outside of themselves to not only cleanse their body but also to cleanse the dark impurities of their hearts. Christianity offers a purification and healing of the heart that Muslims can't get from the ritual washings of Islam. Sharing this can often serve as a lightbulb moment, presenting a solution to their never-ending problem of ritual impurity.

Get Muslims to Read the Bible

Missionaries in Muslim-majority countries affirm that Muslims are often fascinated when exposed to the Bible. They are deeply interested in learning more about the prophets mentioned in the Quran, which offers few details about them. In the Bible, Muslims are intrigued to discover the prophets' full, colorful stories. This is especially the case with Isa al-Masih (Jesus the Messiah).

When Muslims are invited to join a Bible study group, especially one that covers the entire scope of salvation history, things often click for them. They discover God's overarching plan of salvation and how it culminates not with Muhammed but with Jesus. Although some will remain unconvinced, nevertheless exposing Muslims to the Bible has proven to be among the most promising paths to conversion. They might be resistant at first, but a friendly invitation to read the Bible with them is often enough to move forward.

Help Muslims Overcome Works Righteousness

Muslims, like Orthodox Jews, are convinced that the way to earn God's favor is by performing good works. They earn salvation by doing more good things than bad things, by tipping the scale of their life toward the good, but as with the heavy purity requirements, this demand overwhelms Muslims. The high standard presses on them, squeezing them to their breaking point, and when they face it honestly, they know they will ultimately fall short. None of us is capable of being good enough to earn our salvation.

Islam offers no solution to this problem. Muslims are stuck, trying harder and harder to win God's favor, failing and getting frustrated. But Christianity offers Muslims a cure. It tells them that they are saved not because of what they have done but because of what *Christ* has done for them.

When you have an opportunity, you want to share this message with Muslim friends or family members. You can tell them, "You know, you don't have to keep playing the futile game of earning your own salvation. You need someone who is already perfect to bridge the gap between you and God, and that's what Jesus, Isa al-Masih, offers. He's the bridge, and it's by his merits that we find God's favor, not our own."

Expert Interview with Derya Little

➤ **Watch the interview here: https://claritasu.com/little**

Derya Little has journeyed from Islam through atheism to the Catholic Church. She holds a PhD in political science and has written several books, including *From Islam to Christ: One Woman's Path through the Riddles of God*. She lives in a small town in Pennsylvania with her husband and four children.

In this interview, Dr. Little responds to the following questions:

1. What caused you to abandon the Islamic faith of your youth and become Catholic?
2. What do you think Christians most often misunderstand about Islam?
3. What are the main things we should focus on in conversations with Muslims?
4. What advice do you have for Catholics who feel nervous about broaching the topic of Islam?
5. What have you seen to be an effective approach to draw a Muslim into a relationship with Christ?
6. What would you recommend to a Christian who wants to have a good conversation with a Muslim?

Excerpt from the Interview

"So as a Christian, the best thing one can do is to let them start questioning their own beliefs. If you start arguing and discussing about the Trinity and this or that, it's not going to go anywhere because they think Christians changed the Bible and we're just trying to deceive them. There's this deep mistrust.

"So, assign them a saint, pray, fast, and then ask them questions. Try to learn what they believe, so that they can actually start thinking about what they believe. Most Muslims don't even think about what they believe, how they've been taught, whether they are true. It's something they've been taught, and they take it as truth, and never, ever question it. So, bring them to a place of question.

"Another thing, most important, is be a faithful Christian. They need to see the witness of your life. That was such a big turning point for me to see beautiful Christian marriages and families on display." (Derya Little)

ANSWERING THE BEST OBJECTIONS

When you discuss Islam with interested people, you will encounter a number of big objections. Let's consider five of them and how to respond.

Objection 1: "Christians and Muslims don't worship the same God."

Many smart, good-hearted people find themselves on either side of this question, whether Muslims and Christians worship the same God. Let me explain why I take the view that they do, even if their concepts of God are dramatically different.

Let me use an example borrowed from a podcast by Francis J. Beckwith,[2] whom you met in the expert interview for the previous chapter on relativism. Suppose you come home one day and try to push open your front door, but it only opens a few inches because something is blocking it from behind. You push and shove, but nothing works. The thing behind the door is just too heavy and strong. So, you call your neighbor to come and help push. You both shove against the door, but again to no avail. You say to your neighbor, "Wow, what is blocking this door? I'm guessing it's our big dog, if he would only move." But your neighbor replies, "I don't know. It feels like something bigger than a dog. I think someone pushed a couch against your door."

Now, you and your neighbor have different beliefs about what is behind the door—a dog, a couch, maybe something else—however, and here's the key point, they're both describing the same thing. If we asked you and your neighbor, "Are you both referring to the same thing, the thing behind the door?" their answer would be yes. Yet despite referring to the same thing, both have different concepts of what that thing is, and both can't be right. It's either a dog, or furniture, or something else, but we can't pretend all those conceptions are equally true.

The same holds with what Christians and Muslims believe about God. Both groups worship the same God, the one, all-powerful Creator of the cosmos, even if we Christians have a different conception about what that God is like. Those differences are important, and we shouldn't gloss over them, but we are nevertheless describing and worshipping the same God.

Objection 2: "There is only one God, Allah, not three gods like Christians believe."

This is the Muslim's main objection to Christianity, which they base on a misunderstanding. Muslims incorrectly assume that Christians are polytheists. However, Christians don't believe in multiple gods. Like Muslims, we believe that there is only one God. The difference is that we believe

God is a Trinity, one God present in three divine persons, the Father, Son, and Holy Spirit.

You can explain this difference to a Muslim by showing that the Quran itself resembles a trinity. Muslims believe (1) that the Quran is the literal, eternal Word of God; (2) that the Quran has always existed in heaven, but only began to exist on earth when Allah dictated the Quran to Muhammed; and (3) that then it began to exist in book form.

This parallels what Christians believe about Jesus, whom the scriptures call the Word of God that has existed from all eternity. However, instead of merely becoming a book, like the Quran did, the Word became a person, Jesus Christ. This doesn't imply that a Christian believes in two gods (God and Jesus, the Word of God) any more than a Muslim who believes in the Quran thinks there are two gods (Allah and the Quran, the Word of Allah).

In any case, the Trinity is hard enough for most Christians to conceptualize, but it's extremely difficult for people steeped in a unitarian religion, such as Judaism or Islam. Therefore, it's usually best to deflect questions about the Trinity until you're able to make headway elsewhere. Where possible, save this topic for more advanced conversations.

Objection 3: "Jesus never died on the Cross, and therefore he never rose from the dead."

The Quran clearly states this view, which is one of the strangest teachings of Islam:

> [The Jews say], "Indeed, we have killed the Messiah, Jesus, the son of Mary, the messenger of

> Allah." And they did not kill him, nor did they
> crucify him; but [another] was made to resemble
> him to them. And indeed, those who differ over
> it are in doubt about it. They have no knowledge
> of it except the following of assumption. And they
> did not kill him, for certain.[3]

As explained earlier in this chapter, some Muslims interpret this text as saying the person killed on the Cross in Jerusalem was an imposter, possibly Jesus' secret twin brother or someone God miraculously transformed to look like Jesus. Some Muslims even claim the imposter was Judas Iscariot or one of the other apostles. Other Muslims reject this substitution theory and interpret the passage to mean that Jesus was in fact crucified, but that he only appeared to die on the Cross. After he was taken down, he was eventually revived.

These theories are so conspiratorial and lacking in evidence that not a single, serious historian or New Testament scholar, even non-Christians, takes them seriously. Overwhelming evidence shows that the person crucified in first-century Jerusalem really was Jesus of Nazareth and that he really died on the Cross. We have multiple, independent, first-century accounts corroborating this fact, which explains why even John Dominic Crossan, a skeptical New Testament scholar, admits that, "Jesus' death by crucifixion under Pontius Pilate is as sure as anything historical can ever be."[4] Likewise, Gerd Lüdemann, a leading atheist biblical scholar, says, "Jesus' death as a consequence of crucifixion is indisputable."[5]

So, the answer to this objection is that Jesus did, in fact, die on the Cross.

Objections 4 and 5: "Islam is a religion of violence!" and "Islam is a religion of peace!"

You have probably heard both of these claims about Islam. Which is right? Is Islam fundamentally violent or peaceful? The honest answer is both. When we read the Quran, we see both sides on display. For example, some parts of the Quran permit and even encourage violence against non-Muslims, while other parts say non-Muslims should be treated peaceably and with respect. Although such texts are obviously in conflict, few Muslims see a problem with the Quran contradicting itself because, again, Allah is not bound to laws of logic. So, violent Muslims embrace verses promoting aggression and holy wars, while peaceful Muslims emphasize those that encourage respect and peace.

That being said, we can't ignore the history of Islam, which has almost always spread through violence. With the exception of Indonesia and Bangladesh, all Islamic countries have been converted through military force, and we're all aware today of the regular outbursts of Islamic terrorism and violence, especially in the Middle East and Africa.

Some people may contend that Christians suffer from the same charge, since the Bible also advocates violence. The difference is that the Old Testament describes violence prescribed in specific places, at specific times, in response to specific evils. In the New Testament, Jesus clearly advocates peace.

But Islam makes none of these distinctions. The Quran generally permits violence, without qualification, against non-Muslims who resist Islam. And Islam never reforms violent impulses into peace.

TALKING TIPS AND STRATEGIES

Now that we've become familiar with the top objections, let's turn to some talking points that will help you carry on effective conversations about Islam.

Tip 1: Don't judge Islam by particular Muslims.

When you talk about Islam, be sure to speak about the religion itself more than particular Muslims who take extreme, minority interpretations of Islamic teachings or even live in contradiction to it. This is fair for any religion. For example, if people were talking to you about Christianity, you would think it unfair if they only spoke about priests who abused young boys, angry fundamentalists who protested funerals, or Christians who are mean, greedy, and hypocritical. You would object that such people who flout Gospel teachings are not fair representatives of Christianity. The same holds for Islam. Be fair when you talk about it.

Tip 2: Discuss Islamic teachings, not events.

Avoid criticizing Islam by citing examples of violence, such as its spread through military conquest or the numerous examples of Muslim terrorism today. Otherwise, your conversation partner will likely bring up equally bad stories of

Christians committing violence throughout history and the discussion will go in circles and end in a stalemate.

Instead of specific events, focus on the ideas and teachings of Islam that permit violence. Let me give you three examples from the Quran:

- "Fight those who do not believe in Allah" (9:29).
- If people leave Islam, Muslims should "seize them and kill them wherever they find them, and take not from among them a friend or a helper" (4:89).
- "The punishment of those who wage war against Allah and his apostle [Muhammed] . . . should be murdered, or crucified, or their hands and their feet should be cut off on opposite sides, or be exiled" (5:33).

These passages clearly permit and even require violence against non-Muslims. So, you might consider raising these commands to your conversation partner and ask if certain parts of the Quran really advocate violence against non-Muslims. Based on these passages the answer is unequivocally yes, and that should be troubling to any Muslim or pro-Islamic friend who holds that Islam is a religion of peace.

Tip 3: Don't exaggerate the similarities or differences between Christianity and Islam.

You typically see both of these extremes when people discuss Islam. For example, it's true that Muslims worship the same God as Christians, with the qualifications we discussed earlier. But they reject the Trinity, they deny that

Jesus is God, they don't believe that God's essence is love, and they don't trust what the Bible says about God. So, there are major differences that we shouldn't dismiss.

But you can balance these observations by noticing things Muslims and Christians share in common. They typically both stand against secularism, share a similar moral code (excepting the treatment of non-Muslims and women), and reject the damage caused by the sexual revolution. Muslims and Christians both pray often, throughout the day. Notably, Muslims have five sets of required prayers each day, while all Catholic priests, religious, and laypeople who pray the Divine Office (known as the Liturgy of the Hours) do that as well, since it involves praying five sets of prayers throughout the day.

Finally, note that Muslims believe the fundamental attitude toward God is submission, which is also central to Christianity. Every time we say "Thy will be done" in the Lord's Prayer, we are submitting our lives to God. So, be sure to nuance your statements about Islam, and avoid exaggerating the similarities or differences.

Tip 4: Stick to the sources.

Much of what you know about Islam has been filtered through movies, the news, and social media. Few of us have read the Quran, few have devout Muslim friends, and few have studied the history of Islam. As a result, we are not very well-informed about it.

So, you must be extra careful when discussing Islam, especially with Muslims who are already suspicious of

Christians. If you just repeat stereotypical views about Islam that you picked up from television or the internet, you will confirm their doubts.

When you decide to speak critically about Islam, make sure you stick to the sources. Quote a specific passage from the Quran, such as the passages cited above that deny Jesus was crucified (4:157) or the ones that permit violence. If you plan to criticize Muhammed's actions or an episode in Islamic history, be certain you have all the facts. Study the issue carefully before you bring it up in conversation.

Let's summarize the four strategies:

- Don't judge Islam by particular Muslims.
- Discuss Islamic teachings, not events.
- Don't exaggerate the similarities or differences.
- Stick to the sources.

RECOMMENDED BOOKS
(in order of importance)

Andrew Bieszad, *20 Answers: Islam* (Catholic Answers Press, 2016).

I strongly recommend the *20 Answers* booklets from Catholic Answers. They're short, punchy, and accessible. They use a basic question-and-answer format and cover all the main things you need to know. If you pick up this booklet, and read it in about an hour, you will know more about Islam than 95 percent of Catholics.

J. D. Greear, *Breaking the Islam Code: Understanding the Soul Questions of Every Muslim* (Harvest House Publishers, 2010).

Greear, a Protestant missionary who spent many years in Muslim countries, shares practical advice on helping introduce Muslims to Christianity. I should note that he's a deeply ingrained Protestant, and in some places, you'll find expressions of anti-Catholic prejudice. So, for that reason, I don't fully endorse everything in the book. But if you can ignore the 5 percent of biased content, most of it is incredibly useful.

Peter Kreeft, *Between Allah and Jesus: What Christians Can Learn from Muslims* (IVP Books, 2010).

This book is a set of fictional dialogues between Isa, a Muslim college student, and other Christians, professors, and students at Boston College. Dr. Kreeft avoids controversial passages in the Quran and doesn't offer much serious criticism of Islam. I still recommend the book for the similarities it highlights between Islam and Christianity, but it probably needs to be balanced by more critical reading.

Robert Spencer, *Not Peace But a Sword: The Great Chasm Between Christianity and Islam* (Catholic Answers Press, 2013).

A leading Catholic expert on Islam, Spencer argues that Islam and Christianity are much further apart than we may think. As Spencer is quite cynical toward Islam, this wouldn't be the first book I'd recommend to someone, but it's a good counterbalance to books that are more positive toward Islam. The appendix is perhaps the best part of the book, though. It contains the full transcript of a 2010 debate between Spencer and Kreeft on the topic, "Is the Only Good Muslim a Bad Muslim?"

Derya Little, *From Islam to Christ: One Woman's Path through the Riddles of God* (Ignatius Press, 2017).

This memoir shows not only someone converting from Islam to Christianity but it highlights the circuitous path that many people take during such a conversion. Read this book to learn how conversion from Islam to Christianity plays out in a person's life.

FOR REFLECTION AND DISCUSSION

1. Who was Mohammed and how did he develop Islam?
2. Explain the origin of the Quran and describe its content.
3. What are some differences between Christianity and Islam? In what ways are they similar?
4. Why do you think it's difficult to evangelize a Muslim?
5. How would you respond to the Quran's contention that Jesus did not die on the Cross?
6. What is the difference between violence in the Old Testament and violence in the Quran?

FOR PRACTICE

For each of the following scenarios, write a response using what you learned in this chapter.

1. Suppose a Muslim objects that there is only one God as the Jews believed. It's written in Deuteronomy 6:4 (KJV), "Hear, O Israel: the LORD our God is one LORD." Yet Christians call the Father, Jesus, and the Holy Spirit God. That's why Christianity is wrongheaded. Christians say three, but Jews said only one, and Muslims, following them correctly, insist there is only one in the Godhead.

2. Suppose a Muslim questions you, "Why should Christians behave morally and do good works? If Jesus already accomplished the work of salvation, then according to Christianity can't we just behave however we want? According to Islamic teachings, we must always seek to do good works out of obedience and service to Allah."

6

HOMOSEXUALITY

Everywhere you look, especially during the month of June, which has been designated "Pride Month," you'll spot rainbow banners, rainbow bumper stickers, and Gay Pride celebrations. The media has unequivocally declared the normalcy of same-sex relationships. And because of this acceptance, many Catholics are reluctant to express their views. The Catholic Church teaches that people with same-sex attraction are beloved children of God who should be treated with respect, compassion, and sensitivity. Nevertheless, it also teaches that homosexual behavior is intrinsically disordered and thus morally wrong.

Chances are, you will find yourself soon dialoguing about homosexuality with others, especially family members, friends, and coworkers who disagree with the Catholic view. And you will wonder how to communicate the truth to them lovingly and convincingly.

This chapter will give you practical advice for successful conversations about same-sex relationships.

We will cover

- the Catholic Church's teaching about homosexuality;
- common misunderstandings about homosexual behavior;

- two key distinctions that clear up 90 percent of problems in conversations;
- how to engage same-sex-attracted children, relatives, and friends; and
- answers to big objections that advocates make.

WHAT THE CHURCH TEACHES ABOUT HOMOSEXUALITY

Many people are convinced the Catholic Church *hates* people who identify as gay or lesbian or teaches that people with same-sex attraction are inherently evil or hopelessly lost. They're usually surprised to learn none of that is true. Let's look at what the Church actually teaches about homosexuality.

You will find the most succinct summary in the *Catechism of the Catholic Church*, in paragraphs 2357, 2358, and 2359.

Paragraph 2357 outlines the official Catholic teaching:

> Homosexuality refers to relations between men or between women who experience an exclusive or predominant sexual attraction toward persons of the same sex. It has taken a great variety of forms through the centuries and in different cultures. Its psychological genesis remains largely unexplained.
>
> Basing itself on sacred scripture, which presents homosexual acts as acts of grave depravity, tradition has always declared that "homosexual

acts are intrinsically disordered." They are contrary to the natural law. They close the sexual act to the gift of life. They do not proceed from a genuine affective and sexual complementarity. Under no circumstances can they be approved. (CCC, 2357)

Let's unpack the basic facts in this dense text. First, the *Catechism* defines homosexuality as "relations between men or between women who experience an exclusive or predominant sexual attraction toward persons of the same sex." Notice that the passage defines homosexuality solely in terms of *relations*. It's not talking about feelings, dispositions, or attractions. For the Church, homosexuality always refers to sexual *relations* between two people of the same sex.

Second, the *Catechism* observes that homosexuality has been present throughout many centuries and cultures, "in a great variety of forms," but that its origin is largely unexplained. So, the Church takes no position on the cause of homosexual behavior or same-sex attraction. Is it genetic? Is it due to environmental factors, the way that a person was raised, or some combination of those factors? The Church doesn't try to answer those questions since they are beyond its realm of expertise.

Finally, the *Catechism* affirms that homosexual behavior is wrong. It supports this view by referencing both sacred scripture and the natural law. Despite the attempts of some Christians today to twist and reinterpret the very clear biblical condemnations of homosexuality, sexual relations between two men or two women are unequivocally rejected in both the Old and New Testaments.

But if you're talking to someone who supports homosexuality, then they might not accept the authority of the Bible. So, while appealing to the scriptures may be the best approach when talking with a fellow Christian or Jew, quoting biblical texts to others will often lead to failed conversations. For example, if you cite an Old Testament ban on homosexual behavior, the other person might dismiss it as an outdated cultural restriction from ancient times, like the law against boiling a young goat in its mother's milk or wearing clothes made of mixed fibers. And if you refer to St. Paul's words against homosexuality in the New Testament, the apostle might be dismissed as a narrow-minded bigot.

But paragraph 2357 in the *Catechism* offers an alternative position you can use when talking about homosexual behavior. It says that homosexual acts are "contrary to the natural law" and are thus intrinsically disordered. I advise you to base most of your conversations not on the scriptures but on this natural law argument.

How does it work? The idea of natural law originated not with religious people but with ancient Greek philosophers. They recognized that everything in nature has a purpose and that things are rightly used when they conform to it. For example, consider a metal saw. A saw is meant to cut things, such as wood. But if I try to use a saw for something else, like combing my hair or strumming a guitar, not only will I damage the saw but I could seriously hurt myself.

When you use things against their nature, they become dysfunctional and often dangerous.

The same holds for our sexual organs. The male and female genitalia have a definite purpose, which is obvious to anyone familiar with basic anatomy. By themselves, the organs make no sense and are incomplete. They are the only parts of our body that require another person of the opposite sex to justify their existence. This means their purpose is complimentary. They make sense only when combined with the opposite sex organs. When properly used, these organs unite a man and woman at every level of their being—body, mind, and spirit—by coordinating their bodies to a new end, namely procreation.

Understanding the purpose of sex clarifies the *Catechism*'s description of homosexual acts as "intrinsically disordered." This description does *not* mean that same-sex-attracted *people* are inherently evil or psychologically disturbed. The *Catechism* is referring here only to homosexual *behaviors*. Such behaviors are wrong because they are not ordered toward the proper end of the sexual act, and therefore they contradict natural law. Armed with this truth, you can gently correct people who mistakenly claim that the Church regards all LGBT people as disordered. It's homosexual *acts* that are disordered, not people.

In homosexual acts, whether between two men or two women, the sexual organs cannot come together in a unitive, complementary way. Nor is it ever possible for those sexual acts to be ordered toward procreation. And because such behaviors misuse sex in a way that goes against its purpose, they inevitably result in frustration and deep dissatisfaction. People get hurt.

Now let's turn to the *Catechism*'s paragraph 2358:

> The number of men and women who have deep-seated homosexual tendencies is not negligible. This inclination, which is objectively disordered, constitutes for most of them a trial. They must be accepted with respect, compassion, and sensitivity. Every sign of unjust discrimination in their regard should be avoided. These persons are called to fulfill God's will in their lives and, if they are Christians, to unite to the sacrifice of the Lord's Cross the difficulties they may encounter from their condition. (*CCC*, 2358)

Of the three paragraphs in the *Catechism*, this is the one you want to emphasize the most, because it contains teachings most often missed. The Church clearly teaches that people who identify as gay or lesbian must be treated with respect, compassion, and sensitivity. We must avoid any sign of unjust discrimination toward them. So, when someone complains that Catholics speak harshly about those who identify as LGBT, you can apologize for their behavior, explaining that it conflicts with the official teaching of the Church.

Let's look at paragraph 2359, the final of the three passages on homosexuality from the *Catechism*. It says:

> Homosexual persons are called to chastity. By the virtues of self-mastery that teach them inner

> freedom, at times by the support of disinterested
> friendship, by prayer and sacramental grace, they
> can and should gradually and resolutely approach
> Christian perfection. (*CCC*, 2359)

This paragraph in the *Catechism* is directed not to Catholics in general but specifically to same-sex-attracted people, who are wondering how to live a faithful Catholic life in light of their attractions. The *Catechism* says that people with homosexual inclinations, like any person with disordered attractions to food or alcohol, can transcend them through self-mastery, friendships, support, and the grace of God.

So, when having conversations about homosexuality, you want to keep in mind these main points of Catholic teaching:

- Homosexual behavior is sinful, but same-sex attractions or feelings are not.
- The Church rejects same-sex behavior not just because of the Bible but with reasons rooted in natural law and concern for the human person, reasons that even nonreligious people accept.
- We must treat same-sex-attracted people with respect, compassion, and sensitivity.
- The Church calls same-sex-attracted people to chastity and self-mastery, which they can achieve through prayer, grace, and true friendship.

TWO KEY DISTINCTIONS

In any conversation about homosexuality, you want to make two important distinctions as soon as possible in the dialogue. First, distinguish between people's identity and their actions. Second, distinguish between same-sex attraction and homosexual behavior.

Emphasizing these two distinctions will defuse 90 percent of the tension in most conversations. As we have noted, most people think that the Church hates LGBT people or condemns all same-sex-attracted people to hell. They hold these beliefs because they think if you disagree with someone's actions, you must hate the person. And they don't distinguish between homosexual behavior and same-sex attractions, which are often unintentional and unwanted and therefore not sinful.

Distinguish Identity from Actions

First, you must distinguish between people's identity and their actions. In our culture it's common to think that you are what you do, that your actions define your core identity. For example, a person might say, "I'm a basketball player. I train and play basketball from morning to night. It's what I do, it's who I am." But that creates a problem when someone says, "I don't really like basketball. It's so boring." The basketball player, so invested in his identity as a basketball player, may take that comment as a personal attack. He will equate any rejection of basketball with rejection (or even hatred) of him as a person.

People fall into the same confusion with homosexuality. Same-sex-attracted people adopt identity labels such as "gay" or "lesbian." The LGBT culture encourages them to consider their sexual attractions as their fundamental identity. Therefore, when someone expresses even a slight disagreement with homosexual behavior, many regard this as a personal attack and become hurt and upset.

So, as a first move when discussing homosexuality, you should confirm that sexual attraction or behavior does *not* define a person's identity. You can say, "Your sexual orientation doesn't define who you are. Your real, fundamental identity is that you're a son (or daughter) of God, who loves you." Just as you would not introduce yourself as a heterosexual, as though that label defined you, you need to help same-sex-attracted people to distinguish between their sexual attractions and their identity.

Distinguish Attraction from Behavior

The second important distinction involves the difference between same-sex *attraction* and homosexual *behavior*, two things people frequently equate. Same-sex attraction is often unwanted, and as the *Catechism* affirms, its origin is largely unexplained. We don't know why people are sexually attracted to others of the same sex. But we do know that same-sex-attracted persons usually do not choose that orientation. And where there's no choice, there's no sin. The Church recognizes same-sex attractions as disordered, which means they're not aimed or ordered toward the right end, but the Church does not regard these attractions as sinful and does not condemn anyone who experiences them.

Homosexual *behavior* is a different story, though. We choose our actions and thus we are held morally responsible for them. Homosexual behavior is problematic—Catholics would say sinful—because it misuses the sexual act. Just like the abuse of any body part, it will inevitably lead to bad results: physical or emotional pain, dissatisfaction, spiritual unfulfillment, and more.

These distinctions can often bring relief to same-sex-attracted people, especially those with unwanted attractions. Many have wrongly believed that the Church condemned them for their inclinations. They thought that the Church rejected them as persons because it rejected some of their sexual behaviors. Making these two key distinctions affirms that the Church doesn't condemn them but rather offers grace, sensitivity, and support.

TALKING WITH SAME-SEX-ATTRACTED LOVED ONES

You may not have a family member, friend, or coworker who identifies as gay or lesbian, but you likely will soon. The following five strategies contain tested advice that you will find helpful in conversations with them.

Don't Treat Them as Lepers

The laws of ancient Israel required lepers to keep their distance from everyone else. They were shunned because their disease was contagious and contact with them made others unclean, both physically and spiritually.

Don't treat same-sex-attracted people that way. Don't be afraid of them, don't avoid them, and don't treat them like outcasts. Relate to them as you would to any other friend or family member. Smile, joke with them, and exchange small talk. Keep in mind that almost everyone else in your life commits sins that you disagree with, yet you're still friendly and loving toward them. Do the same with your same-sex-attracted loved ones.

Love Them with Concrete Actions

Same-sex-attracted persons have often been deeply wounded by people they love, including friends and family members. Psychologists have observed a strong correlation between male homosexuality and dysfunctional relationships between boys and fathers. Many same-sex-attracted women had awful mothers who ignored them, belittled them, or even abused them.

Loving such a wounded person can be very powerful and healing. Many same-sex-attracted people feel that their orientation makes them unlovable. Show them otherwise. Make your love concrete and tangible. Give them an unexpected gift or compliment. Go out of your way to help them. Affirm their value and your care for them. You want them to see that you love them regardless of whether you agree with their lifestyle.

If you denounce their behavior harshly and immediately, you will lose their trust and attention within seconds.

Correction should come only after you have established a bond of love and trust. First, they need to hear that you care about them, value them, and love them unconditionally. Only then will they be willing to discuss their sexual orientation with you.

Don't Bring Up Their Homosexuality—Let Them

Don't rush to make a loved one's homosexuality a topic of conversation. Let them bring it up in their own time. Now, you want to be ready to discuss it when that time comes, so don't cower. Summon your resolve and push through any difficulty or awkwardness. But wait to broach the subject until they're ready.

Speak Your Beliefs Explicitly

As a Catholic, you agree with the Church that all sexual activity outside of marriage is wrong. That includes not just homosexual activity but also premarital sex, adultery, and masturbation. At the same time, you love and care for your same-sex-attracted child, relative, or friend, and you want the best for them. You want them to find genuine happiness.

Many people feel torn between those sentiments. They say, "I just wish my daughter knew I'm against homosexuality but also how much I love and support her." The way out of the tension is to put those feelings into words. Say exactly what's expressed above. Affirm that you're convinced homosexual activity is wrong but also that you love and support them.

You want to communicate this with your loved one at the right time, prudently, delicately, and with love and compassion. Confirming your love for someone doesn't condone their lifestyle, just as loving someone addicted to drugs doesn't mean you support their drug habit—in fact, just the opposite!

But don't hide your convictions or beliefs. A same-sex-attracted friend told me that what bothers him most is friends that won't speak candidly to him as they would to other loved ones. They hide or soften their convictions. So, affirm your love, but speak your beliefs explicitly. That transparency and authenticity will help build a bridge of trust.

Pray and Fast for Them

This is the foundation beneath the other tips and strategies. You can't do anything more significant for your loved ones, whatever sins they struggle with, than pray for them daily and fast regularly. For example, skip a meal and offer it as a prayer for a same-sex-attracted loved one, asking for healing and wholeness.

If that's all you do, even if you don't try any of the other strategies, you will see changes. You will become more confident and get better at speaking the truth in love, but you will also notice small shifts in your loved one.

Expert Interview with Fr. Philip Bochanski

► Watch the interview here: https://claritasu.com/bochanski

Fr. Bochanski is the executive director of Courage, the leading Catholic apostolate ministering to people with same-sex attraction. He is the preeminent expert on dealing with homo-sexuality and the issues surrounding it.

In this interview, Fr. Bochanski responds to the following questions:

1. How did you get involved with helping same-sex-attracted people and what brought you to Courage?
2. What does your typical day look like? Do you work directly with same-sex-attracted men and women?
3. How would you present the Church's teaching to a same-sex-attracted person?
4. What are some of the biggest misunderstandings about homosexuality?
5. How should we relate and talk with same-sex-attracted family members or friends?
6. What one piece of advice would you give Catholics for discussing homosexuality?

Excerpt from the Interview

"The Church doesn't pass judgment on where [same-sex attrac-tion] comes from or what it's all about. There's not a one-size-fits-all explanation, but we say these are emotional responses to people, to attraction, that are not sinful in themselves. It's never a sin to feel a feeling. But we have to be prudent, and if you're feeling an attraction towards someone who can't be a spouse, or someone of the same sex, then it's best to try to leave that attraction to one side, focus on chaste friendships, focus on understanding the context and the purpose of sex, and that there's more to love than just sexual love. Hand those things over to the Lord and ask him to expand our understanding of what he wants us to do." (Philip Bochanski)

TALKING TIPS AND STRATEGIES

This advice will prepare you for conversations with anyone about the topic of homosexuality.

Tip 1: Don't imply that your objection to homosexuality is arbitrary.

Don't indicate that it's just your personal feeling or opinion that homosexual behavior is wrong or that it's some arbitrary teaching of the Church. The other person will just swiftly dismiss you.

Instead, show how your rejection of homosexual behavior isn't based on personal sentiment or religious arguments. Affirm your good reasons for thinking it's problematic and show that your view is not arbitrary, including some of the reasons form this chapter.

Also, don't use "belief" or "feeling" statements. For instance, don't say, "Well, I just personally believe . . ." or "Well, I just feel that. . . ." The moment you start a sentence like that, the other person will dismiss your views, convinced that you're not proposing a fact that is true for everyone, everywhere. Instead say, "Homosexual behavior is problematic because . . ." or "Homosexual activity is wrong because it distorts the purpose of sex."

If all you do is trade in opinions, you'll get nowhere because the other person will put forward opposite opinions that support homosexual behavior, and you'll end up in conversational gridlock.

Tip 2: Emphasize the distinctions.

Emphasize the two key distinctions from this chapter: first between people and their actions, second between attractions and behaviors. When you are accused of hating or condemning LGBT people, point out that you're not judging *them*, just asserting that homosexual *activity* is wrong. You are applying the Christian teaching that directs us to hate the sin but love the sinner.

Many LGBT advocates will push back and claim you can't separate sexual behavior from identity. They think their actions define who they are. But you should gently disagree. Explain that while you're convinced homosexual behavior is wrong, you still love friends who identify as gay and lesbian and don't condemn them.

You should also emphasize the key moral distinction between same-sex *attraction* and homosexual *behavior*. Point out that same-sex attraction is often unwanted and comes from hazy origins. Be sure to clarify that it's not sinful. However, a person *chooses* to participate in homosexual activity. It doesn't come from a person's genes or environment. It is a choice, and the person who engages in homosexual activity is morally responsible.

Tip 3: Know some resources to recommend.

Because homosexuality is such a complex and loaded topic, it's hard to make immediate headway in conversations. So, you should be prepared to connect people to resources they can pursue later on, privately and at their own pace. That way they don't feel put on the spot and pressured to change their views immediately.

Among my favorite resources are two beautiful thirty-minute films about same-sex attraction from a Catholic point of view: *The Third Way* and *Desire of the Everlasting Hills.* You can find both online. Both are excellent and include interviews with same-sex-attracted men and women who left an active gay lifestyle to find freedom, chastity, and spiritual friendship.

Another valuable resource, especially for parents and pastoral ministers, is a compassionate and practical document released by the US Conference of Catholic Bishops in 1997 titled "Always Our Children: A Pastoral Message to Parents of Homosexual Children and Suggestion for Pastoral Ministers." If you have a same-sex-attracted loved one and are wondering how to relate, I highly recommend it.

Finally, several good organizations minister to same-sex-attracted people. Courage, led by Fr. Philip Bochanski, interviewed above, is an apostolate recognized and promoted by the US bishops that unites same-sex-attracted men and women to each other in supportive friendships. A sister ministry, Encourage, supports the loved ones of people with same-sex attraction—parents, grandparents, spouses, and others. Also check out Eden Invitation, an excellent ministry offering retreats, community, and book discussions for people with same-sex attraction.

ANSWERING THE BEST OBJECTIONS

Now that you better understand homosexuality and how to talk about it, the next step is to get familiar with some of the commons slogans and objections you'll hear from people who disagree. Let's look at five of them.

Objection 1: "You're just a homophobe!"

This is a common slur, but when it comes your way, gently deny that you're not a homophobe because you don't hate same-sex-attracted people and you're not afraid of them.

You might also counter volley by asking, "Would you consider yourself an alcoholic-phobe just because you think alcoholism is wrong and unhealthy? Of course not. Just because we think a particular behavior is wrong doesn't mean we hate or shun people who fall into that activity."

You also want to show that even if that accusation were true, it's irrelevant to the question of homosexual behavior. Even if you *were* a homophobe, that says nothing about the morality of homosexual acts. Philosophers describe this type of name-calling as an ad hominem objection, one that attacks a person's character as a way of sidestepping the argument. For example, it would be ad hominem to deny that two plus two equals four simply because Adolf Hitler claimed it was four, and he was clearly an awful person. Well, he was indeed an awful person, but that has nothing to do with the mathematical truth of two and two equaling four. That statemen is true regardless of whether it's voiced by Hitler or Mother Teresa. The same holds true for moral facts. Actions are right or wrong regardless of who affirms them, so the charge of "homophobia" is simply a distraction.

Objection 2: "You say that homosexuality is unnatural, but that's not true because it's found all over nature. It's totally normal and natural."

Some people observe that homosexual activity has been documented in more than five hundred animal species. From this, they infer that it must also be morally acceptable for human beings. If it's found in nature, it must be natural.

There are a couple problems with this type of reasoning. First, that animals do something doesn't mean it's natural for human beings. For instance, it's also well-documented that many animals eat their own children, but we human beings would never say cannibalism is natural or normal.

Second, there's a confusion about the word *natural*. When we say, "Homosexual behavior is unnatural," we don't mean it's not found in nature or that it's uncommon. The word *unnatural* is being used here in the philosophic sense of "not according to a thing's proper nature or purpose." Homosexual behavior is unnatural because it goes against the obvious nature of the sexual organs. Even a youngster can look at the male and female body parts and understand how they're supposed to come together. The purpose, or nature, of the sexual organs is the conjugal act that unites the man and woman and generates new life. That's the proper nature of sex.

Objection 3: "God made me this way, and God doesn't make mistakes."

If a same-sex-attracted person claims that God made them with their attractions and therefore they're good, you can admit it's true, in a sense. God made each of us exactly as we are, since God is responsible for everything that exists. However, that doesn't mean each of us is without defects in our bodies, minds, or personalities.

Even though God doesn't make mistakes in the sense that he doesn't do something he wishes he hadn't done, he still permits imperfections in our bodies and minds to encourage growth in virtue. For example, God may have made you with a challenging blood disease, or perhaps you have a mental condition that makes it hard to understand complicated subjects. In any case, these imperfections are not good in themselves, but they can produce good effects by offering an opportunity to grow in certain virtues, such as perseverance, humility, reliance on God, and more. Same-sex attraction falls into a similar category.

Objection 4: "The Bible only rejects same-sex behavior between men and boys, or other abusive sexual relationships. It says nothing about loving, committed, same-sex relationships between two adults."

A growing trend, especially in Protestant circles, reinterprets verses of the Bible dealing with homosexuality so that they don't condemn what advocates describe as healthy, loving same-sex relationships. This objection is rooted in major confusion about the Bible. Both the Old Testament and the New Testament unequivocally condemn homosexual behavior. The scriptures make no distinction between abusive homosexual relationships or relationships between two committed adults. It says without qualification that it's contrary to God's plan for a man to lay with another man or a woman to lay with another woman.

But you should add that Catholics don't reject homosexual behavior only because the Bible says it's wrong, although it definitely does. We also reject homosexual acts because they contradict the natural law, the nature of sex.

Objection 5: "Didn't Pope Francis say, 'Who am I to judge?' in reference to gay and lesbian people?"

If there's one thing even non-Catholics know about Pope Francis, this is it. But it must be understood in context. Pope Francis was asked in a question-and-answer session about a man who worked at the Vatican, who had active homosexual relationships before he repented and started working for the Church. The pope's point was that, now that this man has apparently repented, who am I to judge him?

The pope was not endorsing homosexuality or same-sex marriage. He was not saying we shouldn't judge the morality of homosexual *acts*. He was not changing or overturning Church teaching. He was simply affirming that he was not in a position to judge the state of someone's soul, especially when they seemed to have repented of past sins.

You can actually use this exchange as an example, showing people the difference between judging a *person* and judging a particular *action*. Like the pope, we shouldn't judge *people*, but we can determine that an action is wrong.

RECOMMENDED BOOKS
(in order of importance)

Fr. Michael Schmitz, *Made for Love: Same-Sex Attractions and the Catholic Church* (Ignatius Press, 2017).

> This is a sensitive book aimed at same-sex-attracted persons, their family, and their friends. Fr. Mike lays out the Catholic view of love and sexuality, showing how the true nature of love aligns with the sexual teachings of the Church. And he explains how to live out those teachings through chaste friendships and self-mastery.

Glenn T. Stanton, *Loving My (LGBT) Neighbor: Being Friends in Grace and Truth* (Moody Publishers, 2014).

> Stanton, an Evangelical Protestant, explains how to love, befriend, talk with, and respect people who identify as gay or lesbian. This practical book shows ways to navigate tough situations and conversations at home, church, work, and school. An especially good chapter focuses on Christians who model these relationships well.

Fr. John Harvey, *Homosexuality and the Catholic Church: Clear Answers to Difficult Questions* (Ascension Press, 2007).

Fr. John Harvey was the founder of Courage and worked with thousands of same-sex-attracted men and women. This solidly orthodox book is the best presentation of the Catholic Church's teaching on homosexuality. The question-and-answer format includes 110 entries that cover the topic extensively.

Trent Horn and Leila Miller, *Made This Way: How to Prepare Kids to Face Today's Tough Moral Issues* (Catholic Answers Press, 2018).

This is a must-have book for Catholic parents and teachers on today's main moral questions. It contains an excellent chapter on talking about homosexuality with both young children and teenagers.

FOR REFLECTION AND DISCUSSION

1. What reasons can you give to show that homosexual behavior is wrong?
2. Explain why same-sex attraction is not sinful in itself.
3. How can distinguishing identity from actions reduce tension in conversations?
4. What advice would you give to parents who want to have a conversation with a child about homosexuality?
5. How would you respond to someone who accuses you of being a homophobe?

6. What do we mean when we say that homosexuality is unnatural?

FOR PRACTICE

For each of the following scenarios, write a response using what you learned in this chapter.

1. Suppose a friend who supports homosexual behavior says, "Jesus said, 'You shall know them by their fruits.' If a homosexual couple is bearing good fruit in a loving, monogamous relationship, who are you to say that what they're doing is wrong? You're not only wrong but you're going against what Jesus says."

2. A friend or relative says, "The Church needs to get with the times. Homosexuality is natural and found all over the animal kingdom. What's unnatural is to force people to suppress their own sexuality or try to change their orientation. That's why homosexuals commit suicide. The Church is to blame for their horrendous, backward views."

7

MARY

As I went through the process of becoming Catholic, I faced many difficulties—the faith-works stumbling block, the pope, the saints, and purgatory. But the biggest challenge for me was Mary. I didn't understand why Catholics emphasized her so much, especially since she seemed to be a minor figure in the Bible, appearing only a few times in the New Testament. Catholics seemed to elevate Mary next to Jesus, to revere her almost to the point of worship, and to pray to her more than they prayed to Jesus.

But then I read Catholic books explaining this devotion and met Catholics who knew and loved Mary—and I had a Marian epiphany. I not only welcomed Mary, I also grew to love her myself and wanted to help others love her, too.

That's what this chapter will do for you. It will prepare you to talk about Mary with people who don't understand her.

We will cover the following topics

- why Mary is so controversial;
- the key to understanding Mary;
- Mary's role in God's plan of salvation;

- understanding the four Marian dogmas; and
- how to respond to big objections to Mary.

WHY IS MARY SO CONTROVERSIAL?

Why is Mary such a lightning rod? Why do many non-Catholics recoil when they hear her name, see a statue of her, or observe someone praying the Rosary? There are four major reasons why.

First, many Protestants think you have to choose between Jesus and Mary. For them religious devotion is a zero-sum game. You can't devote yourself to two things at once; the more you're devoted to one, the less you're devoted to the other. Therefore, many Protestants think devotion to Mary comes at the expense of Jesus. The more Mary is honored, the less Jesus is honored. And since Jesus deserves the highest honor, Mary should receive little if any focus.

Second, many non-Catholics see exaggerated Marian piety, especially in Latin American countries, and rightfully become alarmed. Although it's not true of all Catholics in Latin America, in some areas, veneration shown toward Mary drifts into superstition or worship. Protestants recoil at this and regard it as the inevitable outcome of *any* Marian devotion.

Third, many have a problem with Mary simply because Marian devotion is identified with Catholicism. This reason alone is enough for many Protestants. They stay away from the Rosary, statues of Mary, processions, and feast day celebrations because they don't want to be involved with anything Catholic.

Fourth, most Protestants follow *sola scriptura*, which means the Bible is their ultimate source of authority. But if you embrace that view, at first glance Mary hardly seems like a major figure. Other characters such as Peter, John, and Paul get far more attention in the New Testament. Also, Jesus does not seem to elevate Mary as he does the other disciples. So, for many Protestants, the attention paid to Mary by Catholics seems disproportionate to her presence in the scriptures.

THE KEY TO UNDERSTANDING MARY

So, how do we respond to such misunderstandings? The first step is to get clear in our own minds about Mary's significance, especially in the Bible. Again, most non-Catholics observe that the Bible seems rarely to mention her. But critics often miss a key point of interpretation, namely that we should pay attention not only to explicit references to Mary but also to foreshadowing, symbolism, and prophecies.

Jesus and Mary in the Old Testament

Most Christians are familiar with implicit references to Jesus in the Old Testament, especially among the prophets. For example, in the oft-quoted chapter 53, Isaiah describes a suffering servant, saying, "He was pierced for our sins, crushed for our iniquity. He bore the punishment that makes us whole, by his wounds we were healed" (Is 53:5). Christians immediately recognize that Jesus fulfilled this prophecy.

On the Cross, Jesus was pierced for our sins and crushed for our iniquity, and by his wounds we were healed of sin.

The Church Fathers searched the scriptures, especially Genesis and Exodus, for implicit mention of Jesus. For instance, they saw Christ as the New Adam, who reversed the sin of the first Adam. They regarded Jesus as the New Moses, who led his people out of bondage to sin into the freedom of God's kingdom. In the psalms, they saw Christ as the New King David, who would rule his people with God's favor and lead them in a chorus of right praise.

However, many Christians, including many Catholics, neglect to apply this same strategy to Mary. Just as we look to the Old Testament to understand Jesus, we should look to the Old Testament to understand Mary. In the same way that Jesus is foreshadowed in the Old Testament, Mary is also present.

Typology

Using the Old Testament to illuminate New Testament figures and events is a form of interpretation called "typology." Biblical typology involves looking for types, figures, or foreshadowing in the Old Testament. For instance, Isaiah's "suffering servant," mentioned above, is a type or foreshadowing of Jesus on the Cross. As St. Augustine says, "The New Testament lies hidden in the Old and the Old Testament is revealed in the New." For this reason, Catholics make extensive use of typology.

Few non-Catholics are familiar with reading the Bible typologically. They sometimes make a few exceptions, such as seeing Jesus as the New Moses or Jesus as Isaiah's suffering servant, but Protestants rarely do this with figures other than Jesus. In fact, while I was a Protestant, I remember hearing about just one typological figure besides Jesus, which was John the Baptist, viewing him as the new Elijah. Yet even this was only because Jesus explicitly notes the connection in the Gospel of Matthew: "He is Elijah, the one who is to come" (Mt 11:14). Other than that, we didn't view any other New Testament figure through the lens of the Old Testament, and that explains why we didn't appreciate Mary. I was never encouraged to look to the Old Testament to understand Mary's significance.

If you're talking with people who think Catholics make too much of Mary, emphasize that to understand her, you simply have to explore the Old Testament. When you do, you'll discover how she was foreshadowed from the beginning of God's plan. As Joseph Ratzinger, later Pope Benedict XVI, once said, "The image of Mary in the New Testament is woven entirely of Old Testament threads."[1]

WHO MARY REALLY IS

With that background we can understand Mary by viewing her typologically through the lens of the Old Testament. We will focus on three dimensions: Mary as the New Eve, Mary as the new ark of the covenant, and Mary as the Queen Mother.

The New Eve

We are all familiar with the story of Adam and Eve in Genesis. In short, God forbade the first human beings to eat of the Tree of the Knowledge of Good and Evil. The serpent tempted them, Eve grasped the forbidden fruit, and she and Adam both ate it.

As a result, God cursed the snake with a verse known as the *protoevangelium*—the first good news—"I will put enmity between you and the woman, and between your offspring and hers; they will strike at your head, while you strike at their heel" (Gn 3:15). This is one of the most important passages in the Bible. As a result of the devil's temptation and Eve's sin, God said he will put hostility between the devil and the woman and between him and her offspring. Her offspring will strike at the devil's head, while he will strike at their heel.

The Church Fathers read this verse as pointing to Christ, Eve's eventual offspring. The devil struck his heel by facilitating his Crucifixion and death. But Christ struck the devil's head by rising from the dead, freeing us from the bondage of sin. For this reason, the earliest Christians saw Christ as the New Adam, the one who fulfilled the prophecy by undoing Adam's sin.

So, for the earliest Christians, Christ was the New Adam. However, Mary was the New Eve. The second-century philosopher and apologist Justin Martyr said that the virgin Eve conceived the word of the serpent, resulting in disobedience and death, and the Virgin Mary conceived the Word of God, resulting in obedience and life. In other words, our new mother (Mary) reversed the disobedience of our first mother (Eve). As the liturgical hymn declares of Mary, the "'Yes' on your lips undid the 'No' of Eve," establishing her as the new mother of all the living. So, from the opening pages of Genesis we already see a foreshadowing of Mary's significance in God's plan.

The New Ark

In the book of Exodus, the ark of the covenant was the golden container that God ordered Moses to build, which held the tablets of the Ten Commandments, Aaron's staff, and a jar of manna. The ark had become God's presence among the Israelites, but strangely it disappeared in the second book of Chronicles in the middle of the Old Testament. It was just lost.

In the book of Revelation, however, we read that "then God's temple in heaven was opened, and the ark of his covenant could be seen in the temple" (Rv 11:19). The very next verse says, "A great sign appeared in the sky, a woman clothed with the sun, with the moon under her feet, and on her head a crown of twelve stars" (Rv 12:1). The woman is with child and gives birth to a son who is destined to rule all the nations.

The woman symbolizes the mother of the Messiah and is clearly a depiction of Mary. But notice how Revelation moves seamlessly from describing the ark to portraying Mary, as if the ark and Mary are connected or even equated.

That's why many early Christians saw Mary as the new ark. The original ark of the covenant disappeared in the Israelite wilderness but then reappeared as the new Queen of Heaven. The original ark contained the Law, the staff of the high priest Aaron, and manna, the bread from heaven. Mary, the more perfect ark, contains within her the fulfillment of all three items. In her womb she held Jesus Christ, who is the new covenant, the eternal high priest, and the new bread from heaven. Also, like the ark, Mary became the locus of God's presence. As the angel said, her son would be called Emmanuel, "God with us." So, Mary held the very presence of God within her. Thus, the entire story of the ark in the Old Testament is meant to point to the new ark, whom we discover in the gospels.

The Queen Mother

Mary is the New Eve and the new ark, but she is also the Queen Mother. Revelation 12, cited above, depicts Mary wearing "a crown of twelve stars" as the Queen of Heaven. This means that Mary's role in salvation is not merely honorary. She reigns with her divine son as queen.

The biblical precedent is Bathsheba serving as Solomon's queen mother. None of King Solomon's 700 wives sat at his right hand but only his mother, whom he treated as his queen. The first book of Kings describes Bathsheba bringing a request to Solomon and the king rising to meet her, bowing before her, and then having a throne chair brought to his right side for her (see 2 Kgs 2:19).

Sitting at the king's right hand, the queen mother holds the most important position in the kingdom, second only to the king. That's another reason the earliest Christians reverenced Mary, who sits at the right side of her son. Even more, she holds a privileged closeness to the King—she has the ear of the King—and can bring our requests and petitions to him, just as Bathsheba did to Solomon.

Now that we have a little better understanding of Mary, let's recap those three dimensions. Mary is the New Eve who undid the sin of the first woman. Mary is the new ark holding within her womb the very presence of God, and Mary is the Queen Mother seated at her son's right hand and reigning with him.

So, the next time someone claims that Mary is hardly mentioned in the Bible, you can say, "On the contrary! Mary is the second-most significant figure in the Bible! She's there from beginning to end, from Genesis to Revelation, if you know how to look!"

Expert Interview with Brant Pitre

➤ **Watch the interview here: https://claritasu.com/pitre**

Dr. Brant Pitre serves as Research Professor of Scripture and Theology at the Augustine Institute in Denver, Colorado. He holds a PhD in theology from the University of Notre Dame, where he specialized in the study of the New Testament in ancient Judaism. He's the author of several books, including

Jesus and the Jewish Roots of Mary: Unveiling the Mother of the Messiah.

In this interview, Dr. Pitre responds to the following questions:

1. Can you tell us about the crisis moment when your beliefs about Mary came under fire?
2. Why is it important to study Mary in her first-century Jewish context? Is this how the earliest Christians viewed Mary?
3. Why would Jesus be read typologically, but not Mary, the disciples, or any other New Testament figures?
4. How did the connection between Eve and Mary ground the belief that Mary was immaculately conceived?
5. Why does it matter that Mary remained a virgin after Jesus' birth?
6. Why is it significant that Mary is the new Rachel?
7. What are some tips and strategies you'd recommend to Catholics when talking about Mary?

Excerpt from the Interview

"If the old Adam is created without sin, the old Eve is created without sin, and the new Adam, Jesus, is conceived without sin, then it's fitting that the new Eve, Mary, would also be conceived apart from sin and not under the power of the sin of Adam and Eve. Otherwise, and here's the key, the old Eve would be greater than the new Eve. That's really important. And not just that. If Mary ever committed a single sin her entire life long, the old Eve would be at least equal then, if not greater than the new Eve.

"But that's just not how scriptural typology works. Old Testament pre-figurations are never greater than their New Testament fulfillments." (Brant Pitre)

GETTING THE MARIAN DOGMAS RIGHT

Let's move now from the Bible to the Church's major teachings about Mary. The Catholic Church has defined four main dogmas about Mary. Because most Protestants (and even some Catholics) misunderstand them, we will look at them carefully to get clear on what they do and don't mean.

As a Protestant, I wondered why the Church defined dogmas such as Mary's Immaculate Conception or Assumption. After all, I thought, why were they so important? Why did they even matter? Why did the Church make them binding truths that all Catholics must believe?

But after studying these dogmas, I realized the main reason the Church defined them was because they are *true*. Even if people misunderstand or have problems with them, Marian dogmas are true, and since Jesus wants to lead us to all truth through the Church, they're worth maintaining.

But I also discovered a second reason for these definitions. Marian dogmas are not only about Mary, they are also about Christ. Each of them teach and safeguard important truths about Jesus, so that if you misunderstand facts about

Mary, you'll inevitably misunderstand important things about Christ.

Mary, the Mother of God

Let's start with the first dogma, which is the declaration of Mary as the Mother of God. This occurred at the Council of Ephesus in AD 431, but Christians had honored Mary under that title for centuries before. The council was specifically called to refute the heresy of Nestorius, an archbishop who held that Jesus consisted of two persons, one human and one divine. As a result, Nestorius taught that Mary was mother of only the human person in Christ, not the divine person, and therefore he did not consider her the Mother of God.

To counter this heresy, the council formally declared that Jesus was not two persons, one divine and one human, but one person with two natures. This meant that because Jesus is God, and since Mary is his mother, Mary must be the Mother of God. As the council arrived at this conclusion, the entire Christian community at Ephesus was waiting outside. When they heard this final declaration, that Mary should be known as the Mother of God, they danced through the streets in an all-night celebration.

Why is this title important? Because it protects an important truth about Jesus—that he is God. When people refuse to acknowledge Mary as the Mother of God, they inevitably question Jesus' own divinity.

Mary's Perpetual Virginity

The second major dogma is Mary's perpetual virginity, which maintains that Mary was a virgin before, during, and after she gave birth to Christ. Most Christians agree she was a virgin *before* giving birth, but Catholics also maintain that she remained a virgin *after* Jesus' birth, that she and Joseph lived a celibate marriage, and that Mary had no other biological children. This is an ancient tradition that dates back to the earliest centuries.

A Celibate Marriage?

How could this be? An increasing number of scholars argue that Mary had taken a vow of virginity before marrying Joseph, which was not unheard of at the time. (For the case below, I am relying on our expert Brant Pitre's book, *Jesus and the Jewish Roots of Mary*.[2])

Here's a clue this was Mary's situation. When the archangel Gabriel tells Mary that she will conceive a child, Mary asks how this can be since she doesn't know a man. Given that she was already betrothed to be married, that was a strange question. Imagine going to a wedding shower and telling the bride-to-be that you can't wait to see the beautiful children she and her husband will have, and she says, "But how could that happen?" You would say, "Well, you're going to be married soon and you and your husband will begin a sexual relationship. Why are you surprised that you might have a child?!"

But Mary acts surprised, as if it were impossible to think of having a child with Joseph. Her reply to the archangel

Gabriel makes sense only if she and Joseph were already committed to a celibate marriage. Mary could not imagine getting pregnant, even after marriage, because she was a consecrated virgin. Joseph, her fiancé, had agreed to respect that commitment throughout their marriage.

The Jesus' Brothers Objection

Yet still, even if it's possible Mary had made such a commitment, many people deny her perpetual virginity since the gospels refer to "the brothers" of Jesus. But this common objection is based on unhelpful translations of the scriptures. The Greek word used in the New Testament for brothers (*adelphoi*) can refer broadly not only to blood brothers but also to cousins, nephews, or even other people of your religious community.

For example, in the Septuagint, the original Greek translation of the Old Testament, the same word *adelphoi* is used to describe Lot's relationship to his uncle Abram. The scriptures say that Lot was a "brother" of Abram, even though he was actually Abram's nephew. From a linguistic perspective, the Greek word for brothers means a close relative and doesn't necessarily imply a shared mother or father.

But there's more evidence that the "brothers" of Jesus were not his blood brothers, because the gospels present them as the sons of another Mary, the wife of a man named Clopas. Brant Pitre makes a persuasive case that the "brothers" of Jesus were actually his cousins. Those four cousins—James, Joseph, Simon, and Jude—were the sons of Clopas and "the other Mary." And we know from sources outside the Bible that Clopas was the brother of Joseph, Jesus' father. So, James, Joseph, Simon, and Jude were the sons of Jesus' uncle, making them his cousins. This theory makes sense of all the gospel evidence. It's also confirmed by early Christian writers who maintained that Mary had no other children besides Jesus.

So, Mary remained a virgin before, during, and after the birth of Christ. She was set apart for the sacred purpose of bringing the Son of God into the world.

The Immaculate Conception

Sometimes people confuse the Immaculate Conception with the virgin birth of Jesus, but this dogma refers to Mary's own conception. It affirms that Mary was conceived in her mother's womb free of original sin. It also declares that through God's special protection she never committed even venial (minor) sins.

How was this case? Was it something Mary earned or deserved? No, it was given through sheer grace, earned by the merits of her son, Jesus. It depended on the same eternal sacrifice of Christ that cleans all other Christians from sin. All Christians are freed from original sin by receiving Christ's grace through Baptism. But in this special case, the sacrifice of Christ worked *backward* in time to cleanse Mary of original sin in a preemptive way, since God is not constrained by time.

Some critics object to the idea of Mary remaining sinless because Paul says, "All have sinned and fall short of the glory of God" (Rom 3:23). But we must not understand Paul as saying that *every single person* has sinned. Children below the age of reason are incapable of sinning and, of course, Jesus did not sin. Paul simply meant that the mass of humankind has sinned, not every individual person.

The Assumption

This fourth and final dogma says that Mary was assumed, or taken up, into heaven at the end of her life. It's debated whether Mary died before her assumption or just fell asleep. The Church takes no formal position on that question. It teaches only that by a special grace, the Lord assumed Mary, body and soul, into heaven, similar to how Enoch and Elijah had been taken up before her.

Evidence supporting this doctrine includes the book of Revelation, where Mary appears in heaven in bodily form (see Rv 12:1). It was fitting that, free from all sin, Mary was ready to enter heaven at the end of her life, and that Christ would want her to reign alongside him forever.

So, those are the four major dogmas: Mary as Mother of God, her perpetual virginity, the Immaculate Conception, and the Assumption. Study them, get clear about what they do and don't teach, and you'll be more prepared for conversations about Mary.

ANSWERING THE BEST OBJECTIONS

Next, let's review some of the best objections to Mary so that you won't be surprised when you hear them.

Objection 1: "Catholics worship Mary. Or at the very least, they honor her way too much."

Protestants observe all the Hail Marys, the images and statues of Mary, people crawling on their knees to Marian shrines, people kissing pictures of Mary—and they conclude that Catholics must be worshipping her.

Respond by simply denying the conclusion. Say that Catholics don't worship Mary. You can clarify, "Worship is reserved only for God, and the Catholic Church explicitly condemns worshipping Mary or any other creature." A Catholic worshipping Mary would be guilty of idolatry and acting against Church teaching.

That being said, Catholics do *venerate* Mary, which is different than worship. Veneration is an elevated form of honor, and we honor her because of her special place in salvation history. Mary is the Mother of God, the New Eve, the new ark, and the most powerful intercessor in heaven, since she sits at the right hand of Christ.

So, we venerate Mary, and when we honor her, the Mother of God, we also honor her son, Jesus Christ.

Objection 2: "In the gospels, Jesus himself says that Mary isn't that special."

The objector probably has in mind one of the passages in the Gospel of Luke where Jesus seems to downplay Mary's significance.

For example, someone tells Jesus, "Your mother and brothers are standing outside and they wish to see you." Jesus replies, "My mother and my brothers are those who hear the word of God and act on it" (Lk 8:20–21). A few chapters later, a woman yells out, "Blessed is the womb that carried you and the breasts at which you nursed." Jesus replies, "Rather, blessed are those who hear the word of God and observe it" (Lk 11:27–28).

These verses seem to show that Jesus does not think highly of his mother. But a closer reading shows just the opposite. Jesus is teaching that holiness comes not from family ties but from obedience to the Word of God. No disciple in history exemplified that quality more than Mary. For example, when the archangel Gabriel announced that she would bear the Son of God she accepted the word without hesitation.

So, in these verses, Jesus is not slighting Mary. He is affirming her greatness which comes not from being his mother but from being his most committed disciple.

Objection 3: "The Bible hardly talks about Mary at all, so she must not be that significant."

We have already covered this ground thoroughly above. Although Mary appears in only about half dozen places in the New Testament, when you read the scriptures typologically, Mary emerges as a central figure from beginning to end.

She is prefigured in Genesis where she becomes the New Eve. She is foreshadowed in Exodus as the new ark of the covenant. The book of Isaiah prophesies her giving birth to the Messiah. Throughout the gospels, Mary appears at all phases of Jesus' life—the beginning, middle, and end. In the Acts of the Apostles, at Pentecost, she receives the Holy Spirit with the other disciples. And she's there at the end of the Bible in the book of Revelation, being crowned the Queen of Heaven.

So, Mary is everywhere in the Bible and is undoubtedly a central figure, but only if you have eyes to see her, only if you read the scriptures typologically, beyond the surface level.

TALKING TIPS AND STRATEGIES

Let's tie together all we have learned in this chapter with five tips and strategies to keep in mind as you discuss Mary.

Tip 1: Distinguish between God and Mary.

You already know how to respond to the objection that Catholics worship Mary. Strongly and clearly, make the main point that Catholics don't worship Mary. Worship is reserved for God, and Mary is not God. She is a creature, like the rest of us.

That being said, Catholics do have a heightened reverence for Mary given her special role in God's plan. She was conceived without sin, gave birth to the Son of God, undid the sin of Eve, and she now reigns as Queen of Heaven. We honor her and pray to her, which means we send our requests to her and ask for help, just as we do our friends on earth.

So, you want to emphasize all this right from the beginning, especially if your conversation partner implies that Catholics worship Mary. Mary is not God or a goddess, and we don't worship her. I've been stunned by how many non-Catholics think this way, so nip that notion in the bud as quickly as possible.

Tip 2: Reject overboard Marian devotion.

Many non-Catholics see excessive Marian devotion as borderline worship, concluding that something must be off with Catholic theology. For starters, it can be helpful to *agree* that in some cases Marian devotion has gone too far.

For example, I've personally heard people pray to Mary as if she *were* the Savior. But while Mary did, in fact, play a role in our salvation, since she gave birth to Christ, she is not coequal with God the Father or God the Son, so we would join our opponent in rebuking this sort of misunderstanding.

The person you're talking with might bring up a Catholic they know who *only* prays to Mary but never prays to Jesus or even expresses interest in him. Again, that's another worrisome sign that devotion to Mary has become excessive. Healthy Marian devotion always leads people closer to her son.

In any of those cases, if your dialogue partner expresses reservations about excessive Marian devotion, you can agree and say that you find those things problematic, too.

Tip 3: Focus on typology.

We have emphasized that the best way to fully understand Mary is to use typology, which means looking for types or foreshadowing of Mary in the Old Testament.

You can introduce typology to friends by saying, "You're probably familiar with the places where the New Testament mentions Mary, but did you know she shows up across the Old Testament, too? That she's foreshadowed in Genesis and Isaiah?" This will surprise many Protestants and lead to an interesting conversation.

Tip 4: Show how Marian doctrines are ultimately about Christ.

As many have observed, Mary is like the moon, and all the light she bears is reflected from the Son. This can be an epiphany for non-Catholic Christians. They are often surprised to realize that Catholic doctrines about Mary ultimately illumine something about Christ, and that all devotion toward Mary is finally devotion toward her son.

We've looked at several examples. For instance, we call Mary the Mother of God to secure the fact that Christ is one person, both fully human and fully God. Calling Mary the Mother of God safeguards Christ's divinity. Or we say that Mary was conceived without sin and was assumed into heaven, not because of her greatness but because of Christ's greatness. Christ preserved his mother from sin and raised her into heaven.

Tip 5: Know and love Mary yourself.

As I shared at the start of the chapter, when I was a Protestant trying to learn more about Mary, what made the biggest impression was Catholics who knew and loved Mary as a real person and who were affected for the better by their relationship with her.

The last command of Christ on the Cross was, "Behold your mother." That was his dying request, and it was one meant not just for the apostle John but for all Christians throughout time. Learn about Mary, behold her, pray to her, and ask for her help. The more we know and love Mary, the more we know and love Christ. Your devotion will show people that Mary is more than an abstract historical figure, but a real, living person. The witness of your love for her is the best way to introduce her to them.

RECOMMENDED BOOKS
(in order of importance)

Brant Pitre, *Jesus and the Jewish Roots of Mary: Unveiling the Mother of the Messiah* (Crown Publishing Group, 2018).

Dr. Pitre explains that Catholic beliefs about Mary are not arbitrary but have deeply biblical roots in the

Bible, especially in the Old Testament. He explores Genesis, Numbers, and Isaiah to show how Mary was foreshadowed centuries before her birth. He writes sparkling prose that makes you feel that you're in an Indiana Jones adventure with one page-turning discovery after another. You can recommend this book with confidence to any Protestant.

Tim Staples, *20 Answers: Mary* (Catholic Answers Press, 2016).

Staples, a top Catholic apologist, answers the most common questions about Mary, Marian dogmas, and objections like "Why do I need to have a relationship with Mary?" The booklet includes quotes from the Church Fathers about Mary that confirm the views of early Christians were undeniably Catholic.

Scott Hahn, *Hail, Holy Queen: The Mother of God in the Word of God* (Image, 2005).

In this modern classic, Dr. Hahn introduces readers to typology, the way of reading the scriptures that sees New Testament people and events prefigured in the Old Testament, offering Mary as a preeminent example. I first read this book as a Protestant, and it persuaded me that Mary deserved all the attention and honor that Catholics awarded her.

Fulton J. Sheen, *The World's First Love* (Ignatius Press, 2010).

In this book, Archbishop Sheen reflects on the major events in Mary's life with his unique blend of insight and imagination. He covers theology and apologetics, but his purpose is to help readers grow closer to Mary and get to know her better.

FOR REFLECTION AND DISCUSSION

1. Why do you think Mary is so controversial?
2. What is typology, and how does it help people understand Mary?
3. How would you explain that Mary is the Mother of God to a skeptic?
4. How do the scriptures support the idea that Mary is the New Eve?
5. Why can we say that Marian dogmas protect truths about Jesus?
6. How would you respond to the objection that Catholics worship Mary?

FOR PRACTICE

For each of the following scenarios, write a response using what you learned in this chapter.

1. Suppose a friend objects, "In Matthew 1:25, the evangelist makes clear that Mary and Joseph had no intercourse until Jesus was born. This clearly means they would have had sex *after* Jesus was born. As a result, the doctrine of Mary's perpetual virginity contradicts the scriptures."

2. A friend or relative says, "The problem with Catholics is they spend far too much time on Mary that should be spent on Jesus. Also, they have all of these weird beliefs in Marian apparitions and secrets. It's bizarre and distracting from Christ. I prefer an authentic Christianity where Christ is at the center."

CONCLUSION

Most Catholics would look at the topics covered in this book and decide these are seven issues they hope *never* arise in conversation. But now, having finished this book, you're different. Even if you haven't memorized every tactic and talking point, you're at least ready to discuss these topics without getting nervous or scared. You know the key points, you've met the top objections, and you've learned how to answer them. You now have clarity, and clarity breeds confidence.

However, you likely still need two things moving forward. First, you need a place where you can practice these tips and strategies. It's one thing to read about them in a book. It's different challenge to master and use them in actual conversations, in the real world. That's why I created ClaritasU, which has a vibrant Community area featuring several discussion forums. There, you will join thousands of other Catholics to practice these skills, ask questions, and get feedback. It's like a training ground for Catholics wanting to master the skills in this book.

The second thing you need moving forward is a way to stay up to date on new topics and challenges. Developments in the culture often change how we should approach each of these issues, so you want to make sure you have the latest information and the most effective tactics. You'll also want to get knowledgeable about *new* challenges, ones we haven't covered in this book. Again, that's what you'll find inside ClaritasU. Each week students receive a new video lesson from me, and every couple of months, we begin a new video course on a burning issue, which means you'll never be left with old, outdated information. You'll always be on the cutting edge. You'll know what to say, and how to say it, about all the most important, relevant topics.

So, as we come to the end of this book, I invite you to join me and thousands of other faithful Catholics inside ClaritasU. Join this movement of excited Catholics rising up against timidity and fear and gain the confidence and clarity you need.

Just visit ClaritasU.com and sign up today. See you inside!

NOTES

1. Faith and Science

1. Nicolette Manglos-Weber and Christian Smith, "Understanding Former Young Catholics: Findings from a National Study of American Emerging Adults" (2018).

2. Nicolette Manglos-Weber and Christian Smith, "Understanding Former Young Catholics: Findings from a National Study of American Emerging Adults" (2018).

3. John Paul II, *Fides et Ratio*, http://www.vatican.va/content/john-paul-ii/en/encyclicals/documents/hf_jp-ii_enc_14091998_fides-et-ratio.html.

4. Pius XII, *Humani Generis,* www.vatican.va/content/pius-xii/en/encyclicals/documents/hf_p-xii_enc_12081950_humani-generis.html.

2. Jesus' Resurrection

1. Peter Kreeft and Ronald K. Tacelli, *Handbook of Catholic Apologetics: Reasoned Answers to Questions of Faith* (San Francisco: Ignatius Press, 2009), 186.

2. Robert Barron, "John Dominic Crossan's strange depiction of Jesus," *Chicago Catholic*, March 13, 2011. www.chicagocatholic.com/bishop-robert-barron/-/article/2011/03/13/father-robert-barron-john-dominic-crossan-s-strange-depiction-of-jesus.

4. Relativism

1. Joseph Ratzinger, homily given at *Pro Eligendo Romano Pontifice* Mass, April 18, 2005.

2. George Barna, *Virtual America* (Ventura, CA: Regal, 1994), 83.

3. George Barna, *Virtual America* (Ventura, CA: Regal, 1994), 85.

4. Allan Bloom, *The Closing of the American Mind* (New York: Simon & Schuster, 1987), 25.

5. Plato, *Theaetetus*, in *Complete Works*, trans. M.J. Levett, rev. Myles Burnyeat, ed. John M. Cooper and D.S. Hutchinson (Indianapolis, IN: Hackett, 1997), 152a 6–8.

6. Plato, *Theaetetus*, in *Complete Works*, trans. M.J. Levett, rev. Myles Burnyeat, ed. John M. Cooper and D.S. Hutchinson (Indianapolis, IN: Hackett, 1997), 172a 2–6.

7. See Tom L. Beauchamp, *Philosophical Ethics: An Introduction to Moral Philosophy* (New York: McGraw-Hill, 1991), 39.

8. See Francis J. Beckwith and Gregory Koukl, *Relativism: Feet Firmly Planted in Mid-Air* (Grand Rapids, MI: Baker Books, 1998), 61–69.

5. Islam

1. Andrew Bieszad, *20 Answers: Islam* (Catholic Answers Press, 2016), 11.

2. *Pints with Aquinas* podcast, "Do Christians and Muslims Worship the Same God?" (episode 164, July 30, 2019).

3. Quran, Sahih International translation, sura 4:157–158.

4. John Dominic Crossan, *Jesus: A Revolutionary Biography* (HarperOne, 2009), 145.

5. Gerd Lüdemann, *The Resurrection of Christ: A Historical Inquiry* (Prometheus Books, 2004), 50.

7. Mary

1. Benedict XVI, *Daughter Zion: Meditations on the Church's Marian Beliefs* (San Francisco: Ignatius Press, 1983), 12.

2. See Brant Pitre, *Jesus and the Jewish Roots of Mary* (New York: Crown Publishing Group, 2018), 100–26.

Brandon Vogt is a best-selling and award-winning author, blogger, and speaker who serves as senior content director for Bishop Robert Barron's Word on Fire Catholic Ministries.

Vogt was one of the millennial "nones" when it came to religion until, as a mechanical engineering student at Florida State University, he began a passionate search for truth. That search led him unexpectedly to the Catholic Church in 2008. In 2013, he started StrangeNotions.com, the largest site of dialogue between Catholics and atheists.

Vogt was named one of the "Top 30 Catholics under 30" by FOCUS as well as one of the "Top 30 Catholics to Follow on Twitter." He is the author of ten books, including *RETURN: How to Draw Your Child Back to the Church* and *The Church and New Media. Why I Am Catholic (and You Should Be Too)* won first place in the 2018 Catholic Press Association book awards for popular presentation of the faith. His work has been featured by media outlets, including NPR, Fox News, CBS, EWTN, *America* magazine, Vatican Radio, *Our Sunday Visitor*, *National Review*, and *Christianity Today*. He is a regular guest on Catholic radio and speaks to a variety of audiences about evangelization, new media, Catholic social teaching, and spirituality.

brandonvogt.com
claritasu.com
strangenotions.com

Learn how to discuss the toughest hot button issues!

JOIN MORE THAN 4,500+ CATHOLICS

(including hundreds of priests, nuns, and seminarians!)

Expert interviews on each topic with:

- Dr. Peter Kreeft
- Fr. Mike Schmitz
- Jennifer Fulwiler
- Dr. Brant Pitre

Courses at ClaritasU include:

- Atheism
- Homosexuality
- Transgenderism
- Faith and Science
- Why Be Catholic?
- Heaven, Hell, and Purgatory
- Jesus' Resurrection
- Islam

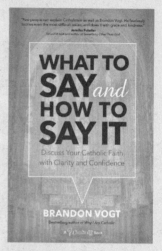
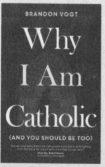